# Hegemony of Homogeneity

JAPANESE SOCIETY SERIES

## General Editor: Yoshio Sugimoto

Lives of Young Koreans in Japan
*Yasunori Fukuoka*

Globalization and Social Change in Contemporary Japan
*J.S. Eades  Tom Gill  Harumi Befu*

Coming Out in Japan:The Story of Satoru and Ryuta
*Satoru Ito and Ryuta Yanase*

Japan and Its Others:
Globalization, Difference and the Critique of Modernity
*John Clammer*

Hegemony of Homogeneity:
An Anthropological Analysis of *Nihonjinron*
*Harumi Befu*

# Hegemony of Homogeneity

## An Anthropological Analysis of *Nihonjinron*

Harumi Befu

Trans Pacific Press

Melbourne

First published in 2001 by
Trans Pacific Press
PO Box 120, Rosanna, Melbourne, Victoria 3084, Australia
Telephone: +61 3 9459 3021
Fax: +61 3 9457 5923
E-mail: enquiries@transpacificpress.com
Website: http://www.transpacificpress.com

Set in CJR Times New Roman by digital environs Melbourne
enquiries@digitalenvirons.com

Printed in Melbourne by Brown Prior Anderson

Distributed in North America by
International Specialized Book Services,Inc.
5824 NE Hassalo Street
Portland,Oregon 97213-3644
USA
Telephone:+1 800 944 6190 (toll free)
Fax:+1 503 280 8832
E-mail:orders@isbs.com
Website:http://www.isbs.com

ISSN   1443–9670 (Japanese Society Series)
ISBN   1-8768-4305-5

**National Library of Australia Cataloging in Publication Data**

Befu, Harumi.
Hegemony of homogeneity : an anthropological analysis of
Nihonjinron.

Bibliography.
Includes index.
ISBN 1 876843 05 5.

1. National characteristics, Japanese. 2. Anthropology -
Japan. 3. Japan - Civilization. I. Title. (Series :
Japanese society series ; vol. 5).
915.2

# Table of Contents

For Kei

# Preface

Academic interest in *Nihonjinron*, Japan's dominant identity discourse, became noticeable abroad in the 1970s. In the 1980s a number of conferences and symposia began to be held on the topic. By now the term is part of the common vocabulary of those who work in Japanese studies. Yet we are not apprised of the full nature of this discourse.

My interest in the topic began in the late 1970s. I became concerned with stereotypic characterizations of Japan in the media, which amounted to Japan bashing at the time. I began to realize that such overseas characterizations of Japan were not entirely the fault of the foreign press – much of the blame was to be laid with the Japanese, as they produced voluminous and monolithic literature on who the Japanese are and what constitutes Japanese culture and society This realization is at the basis of this book, in which I review, analyze, and interpret the way the Japanese characterize themselves.

My first major effort in this direction was a conference I organized in 1978 with the support of the Social Science Research Council at Shakertown, Kentucky, in the United States. The focus of the conference was *Japanese groupism*, which is a central component of this discourse. About this time, I also spoke on Japanese groupism at the University of New Mexico and the Berkeley, Santa Barbara, and Los Angeles campuses of the University of California. I began to publish critiques of the notion of the Japanese groupism and other aspects of *Nihonjinron* from 1980 on. At first, I won very few converts. My first major allies were Yoshio Sugimoto and Ross Mouer in Australia. Their views resonated with mine wholeheartedly, and they invited me in the early 1980s for the inaugural conference of the Japanese Studies Association of Australia and two years later to a special conference in Japanese studies at Noosa Head, where I was able to air my views to receptive audiences.

In the first half of the 1980s I gave papers on *Nihonjinron* at the Centre nationale de recherche scientifique (in Paris, France – where Mary Picone graciously invited me as a research fellow), at a conference on Japan's internationalization at Kwansei Gakuin University, which Mannari Hiroshi and I organized, and at the first of the sixteen annual symposia on Japanese civilization sponsored by the Taniguchi Foundation and organized by Dr. Umesao Tadao, then director-general of the National Museum of Ethnology in Japan. These papers have been published in conference proceedings and other sources.

In 1987, with the generous endorsement of philosopher Tsurumi Shunsuke, a collection of my papers on *Nihonjinron* was published in Japanese and was widely reviewed in mass media because of the interest of the general public in the topic. About this time Kwansei Gakuin professor Manabe Kazufumi and I began a series of collaborative works on *Nihonjinron*, beginning with a questionnaire survey in 1987 and analysis of the data in subsequent summers. Some of the results of this collaboration were presented at the triennial conference of the European Association for Japanese Studies held in Durham, Scotland, and elsewhere, and have been published in Kwansei Gakuin's *Annual Studies* and *Shakaigakubu Kiyō*. Much of the data and analysis in this book derive from this collaborative work. By 1990 I began to think of *Nihonjinron* in relation to the concept of cultural nationalism and ethnicity. I organized a conference titled 'Cultural Nationalism in East Asia' and published its proceedings in a volume I edited.

Opportunities to give courses on *Nihonjinron* at Tübingen and Humboldt Universities in Germany and at Aahus University in Denmark allowed me to receive reactions to my ideas on *Nihonjinron* from European students, which I found to be quite different from those of North American students. They gave me valuable insights and taught me to appreciate diverse ways of thinking about Japan and *Nihonjinron*.

This book is a result of accumulation of ideas that have evolved over the years. These ideas continue to evolve and change. But at the turn of the century and the millennium, this is as good a time as any to pause, take stock, and present them to my English reading audience.

# Acknowledgments

Academic enterprise, like most others, involves much support in diverse ways. I am grateful to all the support extended to me over the many years before this book was completed.

All the opportunities made available to me to present different aspects of *Nihonjinron* have been important in developing and revising my ideas. Such opportunities were given me at the kind invitation of numerous institutions, including the University of New Mexico, the Berkeley, Los Angeles, and Santa Barbara campuses of the University of California, and Tokyo University, where I spoke to the faculty and students. The Nordic Institute for Asian Studies generously arranged a lecture tour through Scandinavian countries for me to speak on Japan, including aspects of *Nihonjinron*, at Bergen, Lund, Gothenberg, Oslo, Stockholm, and Helsinki Universities. Opportunities to speak to Australian audiences were provided with the kind invitation of Yoshio Sugimoto and Ross Mouer in the early 1980s. About this time, Mary Picone kindly secured funds for me to spend a month in Paris to concentrate on research, freeing me of administrative and teaching duties. In Japan my colleague Nakano Takashi used his resources on my behalf to have the academic publishing house Ochanomizu Shobō fund a mini-conference on the group orientation of the Japanese on Lake Yamanaka at the foot of Mount Fuji. Other venues where I was given a forum to present my ideas on *Nihonjinron* include the University of Tampere in Finland, Meiji University, Kwansei Gakuin University, the International Center for Japanese Studies in Kyoto, and Kyoto Jinruigaku Kenkyūkai. I am grateful to all these institutions for allowing me to speak on *Nihonjinron* and to test out my ideas.

I benefited from having time off from my regular duties at Stanford University to concentrate on my research. These leaves were taken at the National Museum of Ethnology, Kwansei Gakuin University, Stanford Humanities Center, and East-West Center in

Hawaii. These leaves also gave me opportunities to present my ideas to diverse audiences and receive their input.

Among the sources of financial support were Social Science Research Council for allowing me to organize a conference on the group orientation in Japan, Stanford University Center for East Asian Studies for hiring research assistants and for funding travel to conferences to present my ideas on *Nihonjinron*, Stanford Humanities Center and the East-West Center for providing time for research on *Nihonjinron*, the Fulbright Hayes fellowship program and the National Endowment for the Humanities for funding time in Japan for collecting material for research on *Nihonjinron*, and Kyoto Bunkyo University's Institute for Cultural and Human Research for its support in the final stages of completion of the manuscript.

I am indebted to numerous people who directly assisted me at various stages of completing the manuscript, among whom are Tominaga Masatoshi, Honda Mari, Fukui Ikuko, and Iiri Makiko, as well as Teshima Keiko for painstaking bibliographic search and Hilary Powers for her patient and superb professional editing of the manuscript.

Finally but hardly the least, I owe special thanks to Yoshio Sugimoto for his encouragement and support to publish the manuscript through Trans Pacific Press.

The last three chapters of this book were updated and extensively revised from papers published elsewhere, as follows:

Chapter Five: 'Symbols of Nationalism and *Nihonjinron*.' In *Ideology and Practice in Modern Japan*, eds. R. Goodman and K. Refsing. London: Routledge, 1992, pp. 26–46.

Chapter Six: 'Civil Religion in Contemporary Japan: The Secular Theology of *Nihonkyo* and *Nihonjinron*.' In *Acta Universitatis Temperensis*, ser. B, vol. 42: *Transient Societies: Japanese and Korean Studies in a Transitional World*, eds. Jorma Kivistö, et al. [Tampere: Tampere University Press], 1993, pp. 18–50.

Chapter Seven: 'Swings of Japan's Identity.' In *Cultural Encounters: China, Japan, and the West: Essays Commemorating Twenty-Five Years of East Asian Studies at the University of Aarhus*, eds. Søren Clausen, Roy Starrs, and Anne Wedell-Wedellsborg. Aarhus: Aarhus University Press, 1995, pp. 241–267.

Japanese names are written with the surname first, followed by the given name. Long vowels are indicated with a macron over the vowel, except for words that are commonly used in English such as *Shinto*, *Tokyo*, and *Kyoto*.

# 1 Japan and the West: Mutual Misunderstanding

Throughout much of the period after the Second World War, Japan has been a target of criticism from the world, in particular from the Western world, over political and economic issues. Public officials, businesspeople, and the media pundits abroad, especially in the United States, have accused Japan of dumping goods, cutting prices unfairly, making much of the Japanese market inaccessible for foreign investment because of its excessive regulations and labyrinthine distribution system, and not giving foreign businesses such as construction fair access to the Japanese market. At worst, Americans and other foreigners have accused Japan of racism, ethnocentrism, and parochialism for keeping economic benefits to itself.

Japan has responded to these criticisms in good part by accommodating the demands, but also in part by accusing Western countries of not understanding the special situation of Japan arising out of its unique history and culture, be it patterns of communication, manners of business negotiation, industrial organization, or government-business relationship. Japanese culture and American culture are obviously different from each other, and cross-cultural understanding does require effort on each side. But the heat seems to be on the Japanese side, having to excuse itself and explain itself. In this effort, Japan has often resorted to 'cultural exceptionalism' as a defensive explanation. Because foreigners accuse Japan, or the Japanese, as a collective entity, the response assumes the same monolithic approach. That is, irrespective of variations within Japan and regardless of differences among the Japanese, Japanese culture is said to have certain uniform characteristics, and the Japanese are supposed to behave and think in a certain monolithic manner. These Japanese responses are drawn from a vast reservoir – well known to most

1

Japanese – of presuppositions and presumptions, propositions and assertions about who the Japanese are and what Japanese culture is like.

## Terminology

This reservoir of knowledge on characteristics of Japanese culture, people, society, and history is often glossed as *Nihon bunkaron*, *Nihonjinron*, *Nihon shakairon*, and *Nihonron*. Literally, these terms refer respectively to propositions about Japanese culture, Japanese people, Japanese society, and Japan itself. However, the terms are used interchangeably rather than to designate distinctive subfields of the genre, and thus a book advertised as a piece in *Nihon bunkaron* (culture) may deal with society and national character, or a book about the Japanese national character (*Nihonjinron*) may be advertised as a piece in *bunkaron* (dealing with culture). Like other popular terms used in everyday conversation, these are vague and nebulous in meaning, given to ambiguity. The whole genre can be regarded as one dealing with Japan's identity, attempting to establish Japan's uniqueness and to differentiate Japan from other cultures. In this book we shall use the term *Nihonjinron* because of its relative prevalence in English parlance, even though in Japanese, *Nihon bunkaron* is the most popular term.

In *Nihonjinron* and other terms in this genre, *ron* translates as 'theory,' 'view,' 'interpretation,' and the like. It does not necessarily, though it might, denote well-researched scholarly theory. For instance, 'evolutionary theory' in biology is called *shinkaron*. None but a small percentage of Nihonjinron propositions can be equated in theoretical sophistication with the theory of evolution. Rather, its more commonsensical usage is notably applicable in this context, where *ron* should be understood to have a broad and vague meaning referring to generalizations, in this case, about Japan, Japanese culture, Japanese society, and the Japanese people, much as the term 'theory' is used in English common parlance.

This ambiguity in the meaning of the term *ron* can become a convenient ploy for *Nihonjinron* writers: an impressionistic essay on Japan without any methodological or scientific rigor, for example, can be legitimately admitted as a *ron* – a piece in *Nihonjin*ron – and then be conveniently understood (or misunderstood, as the case may be) to have scholarly status as a scientific theory. Indeed, there is erudite, scholarly *Nihonjinron*, carried out by scholars in their ivory towers to identify the essence of Japanese culture or society; but the vast majority of discourse in *Nihonjinron* is for popular consumption. In this book we focus on the latter type of *Nihonjinron* because our interest is in examining popular forms of cultural identity – what men and women on the street think about their cultural identity, not what an obscure scholar might write for a small audience of fellow scholars. We shall explore the distinction between these two types of *Nihonjinron* later.

## Quest for Identity

One reason that makes the question 'Who are we, the Japanese?' particularly germane is that most Japanese are themselves very much interested in their national identity and have articulated their interest in a variety of ways, notably in published media, so much so that *Nihonjinron* may be called a minor national pastime.

Search for one's identity is not unusual. The question 'Who are we?' haunts all of us at one time or another. It is a particularly pressing issue in a rapidly changing and complex society where one's identity cannot be simply taken for granted: as society changes, the former definition of self-identity no longer suffices and a new one must be created. Also, the availability of so many alternative lifestyles and values to choose from creates a crisis in identity formation in the postmodern world.

The search for identity may be an individual matter, as when a young woman tries to be independent in a society fraught with male chauvinism or an orphaned man tries to locate himself in a kinship nexus. Or this search may be of a broader, cultural nature. 'Who are the Jews?' or 'What constitutes American-ness?' for example, are recurring questions that generations of Jews or Americans have tried to answer. In this book, the topic is the identity of the Japanese.

Although a more detailed examination is reserved for later chapters, it should be mentioned at least in passing here that

*Nihonjinron* writings share a singular objective: to demonstrate unique qualities of Japanese culture, Japanese society, and the Japanese people. What defines the genre of *Nihonjinron* is the fact that its assertions and generalizations have to do with the nature of Japanese culture in general, society in general, or national character in general. As such, little or no attention is given in writings of this genre to internal variation, whether along the line of region, class, gender, rural or urban settings, or any other criterion. Consequently, broad generalizations of an essentialized Japan abound in this genre.

This book is about *Nihonjinron* in its various guises. It examines the sources of information propagated in this genre, the producers and the consumers, contents of this discourse, validity of the propositions in this discourse, its basic premises, the 'religious' ramifications of *Nihonjinron*, the popularity of this discourse in relation to the demise of symbols of Japan's national identity, and finally the changing nature of this discourse in Japan's modern history.

Let me make it absolutely clear at the beginning. I am not trying to defend any *Nihonjinron* proposition, some of which, such as belief in the importance of 'blood' for learning the Japanese language, are indeed outlandish. Nor is it the purpose of this book to make judgments about *Nihonjinron* writings, as critics like Roy Andrew Miller (1982) and Peter Dale (1986) have done, for example. My purpose, rather, is to analyze *Nihonjinron* as a cultural phenomenon as critically and objectively as I can, in short, to engage in the anthropology of *Nihonjinron*.

Because our concern is how the Japanese themselves create their own identity, how they maintain it, what assertions of uniqueness they espouse, and how they feel about such assertions, we are interested in examining the *Nihonjinron* literature produced by Japanese. That is, we are not primarily interested in foreigners' discourse on the Japanese identity, although many a foreigner has written on the topic. Many indeed have cashed in on this lucrative publishing field through publication of Japanese translations of their works. Once translated, these foreigners' works can be read by any Japanese, and thus such works become part of the genre to be examined here. This situation will be elaborated in Chapter Three, on the literature of *Nihonjinron*.

## Enumeration of Traits

In Chapter Two, we will discuss the all-encompassing nature of *Nihonjinron*. We shall see how wide-ranging its arguments are, some claiming identity of the Japanese through history, some from environment, still others from rural community structure, language, psyche, philosophy, esthetics, and literature. Almost every type of natural and cultural phenomenon is fair game here. We will then review the nature of the literature on *Nihonjinron*. Books are hardly the only source of information. Other media – magazines and newspapers and also electronic media like radio and television – are common sources, as well.

*Nihonjinron* consists of a set of characteristics that supposedly separate the Japanese from other national or ethnic groups. Cultural characterization for *Nihonjinron* – or for any ethnic group for that matter – is necessarily selective. Selectivity is essential to reduce the unwieldy complexity of reality to a manageable summation. One of the crucial questions is what to select and what to leave out.

Selectivity involves conscious decision and is affected by a number of factors external to *Nihonjinron* itself. For example, what traits are selected is a function of what cultures Japan is contrasted with and what cultural traits the Japanese wish to emphasize in contrast to cultures being compared with Japan. For example, a widely circulated 'unique' Japanese trait is the supposed group orientation of the Japanese, which is discussed so often in the *Nihonjinron* literature precisely because it conveniently contrasts with the individualism of the West.

Features chosen to characterize a group must differentiate that group from others, although the differentiation may be only implicit. When Japanese writers mention *amae* (social and psychic dependency on others) or *kotodama* (spiritual quality of the Japanese language) without explicit comparison, they are calling attention to features of Japanese personality or culture that one would presumably not find in other cultures. The assumption is that full meanings of these terms are to be found only in Japanese culture and language. Because only ethnic Japanese speak the language, *Nihonjinron* protagonists can rest assured that these concepts are uniquely Japanese. In other cases *Nihonjinron* traits are picked on the basis of explicit contrast. For example, the rice diet of the Japanese may be contrasted with the meat diet of Europeans (Sabata 1979). Similar contrasts are legion and will be taken up in more detail in Chapters Two and Three.

## Interests at Stake

With whom should Japan be compared and contrasted in deriving its differentiated characterization? This comparison is not random in *Nihonjinron*. It is dictated by Japan's national interest, positive or negative. Economic competition or military rivalry, for example, may be the basis. No purpose is served in distinguishing one's group from groups that have no relationship and nothing to share. Thus in modern times, *Nihonjinron* writers have most frequently compared Japan with Western civilization or one or another Western country, particularly the United States, because Japan's political and economic fate is so heavily entangled in its relationship with the United States.

This is not to say that comparisons with non-Western countries are absent. A few books do compare Japan with China or Korea, but the West is overwhelmingly the principal 'Other' for *Nihonjinron* writers. I have looked far and wide and found no writing in this genre comparing Japan with African countries. Africa, of course, has never mattered much to Japan politically or economically, except only recently and only insignificantly in terms of trade and aid. Economically, technologically, socially, and in any other way, Japan sees little to gain or lose from Africa, and hence has no interest in involving Africa in its effort to create its identity.

It is thus that *Nihonjinron* is by and large built on comparing and contrasting Japan with the West. If some accident in history had made Japan's contrastive referent not the West but the Islamic world or India, *Nihonjinron* would probably concern itself with Japan's monogamous marriage system, which contrasts with Islamic polygamy, or with India's caste system or Hindu spiritualism. Out of such comparisons, *Nihonjinron* writers would no doubt have woven 'unique' patterns of Japanese culture, where Japan would be characterized as a 'uniquely monogamous' society, one lacking a caste system and emphasizing social mobility, or one that is highly materialistic rather than spiritual. It is only because Japan and the West happen to share a similar kinship system (including monogamy), share a materialistic orientation, and lack a caste system that these phenomena are not at issue in the modern *Nihonjinron*.

## Popularity

How popular is *Nihonjinron*? Because of the fuzziness of the concept, a reliable bibliography would be difficult to compile. Fringes of the field are especially difficult to delineate, though its central core is easy to identify. A partially annotated bibliography in this genre was compiled by Nomura Research Institute (Nomura Sōgō Kenkyūjo 1978), but it suffers both from being outdated and not clearly defining the field. It omits many important titles and misses many borderline works. Furthermore, it lists only book-length monographs and omits magazine and newspaper articles.

Be that as it may, it was an attempt to encompass the field, and the only more-or-less comprehensive one, at least up to the date of its publication, that I know of. For the period the bibliography covers (1946 to 1978), it lists 698 titles, and the titles increase in number at a geometric rate from year to year, especially since about 1970. If a similar compilation since 1978 were added to the list, the total would no doubt far exceed a thousand. If articles from periodicals were added, the number would easily multiply by a factor of two or three. Many of the monographs listed have become instant best-sellers or perennial favorites, for example, the Japanese versions of Nakane Chie's *Japanese Society* (1970) and Doi Takeo's *Anatomy of Dependence* (1973), Watsuji's *The Climate* (1961), Suzuki Daisetz's *Zen and the Japanese Culture* (1959), and Isaiah BenDasan's *The Japanese and the Jews* (1972).[1]

## Scholarly and Popular *Nihonjinron*

*Nihonjinron* literature comes in a continuum from the most erudite to the most banal. This fact needs some elaboration. At one end of this continuum are highly scholarly works that attempt to characterize Japanese culture. These technical works are often expensive because of their limited print run and sheer size – often four to five hundred pages – so they do not appeal to the general public. One would not find them in ordinary bookstores. Thus the effects of more erudite works on the general public are indirect; contents of such books are often incorporated in popular books on *Nihonjinron*.

At the other end of the continuum are popular books, which are the central focus of this book. These are the books that fill shelves of popular bookstores, where students and white-collar workers stop in to see if they can pick up a book to read on the home-bound train. What these commuters want is light reading – not a book that requires concentration and cogitation but one that allows fast reading and quick comprehension. It is on the whole these books that are the subject of the discussion in this volume.

## The Role of the Intellectual

Receiving a Nobel Prize is undoubtedly a desired public recognition for scholars all over the world. But the vast majority of scholars in the United States and other Western countries are not motivated to appear on television or radio or to write regularly for newspapers and popular magazines. Although many scholars may be secretly envious of Margaret Mead's or Carl Sagan's popularity with the general public, they at the same time deride such scholars as 'popularizers,' where the term *popularizer* itself has a pejorative connotation. Rather, their orientation is toward educating students and receiving recognition among their academic peers for scholarly achievements.

In Japan, intellectuals have a much broader role among the general populace. They are listened to more seriously by the public, too. Intellectuals who write *Nihonjinron*, then, have significant effects on the population, as Yoshino (1992) discusses in his book.

Yoshino examines how the Japanese conceptualize their own identity. This point should be made clear and emphasized lest misunderstanding result. Numerous foreigners, intrigued by the question of Japanese identity, have written much on the subject. Thus there is *Nihonjinron* by Japanese and *Nihonjinron* by foreigners. The former is a self-portrait, as it were; the latter is a portrait of an Other. Different motives are involved in the two.

One's ego is heavily implicated in a self-portrait, whereas a degree of detachment is possible in portraying someone else. One might criticize oneself or do the same toward an Other, but the motives behind the criticism are quite different depending on whether the object of criticism is the Self or the Other. It should be made clear at the outset that this book is about self-portrait, not other-portrait, and we shall concentrate on what Japanese have to say about themselves.

## *Nihonjinron* and National Symbols

Why is *Nihonjinron* so popular? Why are the Japanese, especially throughout the postwar era, so concerned with the question of their identity? This complex question requires multiple answers. Many factors converge to produce this popularity, and different sets of factors are responsible for the popularity in different times of Japan's modern history.

Inasmuch as *Nihonjinron* is a discourse on the identity of the Japanese, it may not be unreasonable to ask in what other non-discursive ways Japan's identity has been manifested. Here we find symbolic manifestation as a powerful means of expressing the identity of the nation and its people. Until the end of World War II, there were clear and unambiguous symbols in the imperial institution, the national flag, the national anthem, and the national emblem. For numerous reasons to be explored in Chapter Five, in the postwar period these symbols lost the clear and unambiguous status of pre-1945 days. They became tainted by their close association with the now dishonored war effort. It will be hypothesized that the popularity of *Nihonjinron* is in good part attributable to this demise in national symbols as a means of expressing the identity of the nation and the people.

## *Nihonjinron* as Religion

Robert Bellah (1970) and others have argued for the concept of 'American civil religion,' in which American civil values are said to be celebrated on such occasions as Veterans' Day and Thanksgiving. These values are also highlighted in the president's inaugural oath of office and whenever a public official invokes

God for help. 'Religion' here, of course, is understood as a broad, normative orientation, rather than narrowly as a system of belief in the supernatural or the transcendental.

Bellah and Winston Davis have extended this concept of civil religion and applied it to Japan, going back to the prewar era. In Chapter Six, I take up where they left off and further elaborate on the theme by synthesizing Bellah's and Davis's approaches with the concept of 'the religion of Japan (*Nihonkyō*),' as proposed by Isaiah BenDasan (1970) and Yamamoto Shichihei (1997).[2] I argue that the BenDasan/Yamamoto concept – especially its normative ramifications, which I call 'moral imperatives' – is essentially *Nihonjinron*.

## Vicissitudes of *Nihonjinron*

We have no way of knowing what sort of self-identity, if any, the prehistoric Japanese may have espoused, and few sources divulge what the Japanese may have thought of Chinese and Koreans in the seventh and eighth centuries, when the latter brought over their latest and most advanced culture, and how the Japanese may have formulated their *Nihonjinron* in relation to these Others. We can be more specific about more recent times. In the eighteenth century and the first half of the nineteenth century, when neo-Confucianism held sway in Japan as the official scholarship and the political philosophy, the so-called National Learning (*kokugaku*), which emphasized the emperor's central place in Japanese history as well as indigenous Japanese cultural concepts, began to take hold among underdog scholars. Here was a nascent *Nihonjinron* contrasting Japan with China, under whose shadow Japanese intellectuals had lived for so long.

In modern times, however, as we all know so well, the West replaced China as the civilization to contend with and on which Japan's future hinged. It is no wonder, then, that the West became Japan's referent to look up to – the Other whose standards the Japanese were to emulate. *Nihonjinron*, too, now began to be formulated on the basis of comparing and contrasting Japan with Western countries, especially England, Germany, France, and the United States. This pattern has not changed for the past 150 years.

But there have been ups and downs in *Nihonjinron*, sometimes riding high when the country's mood was nationalistic and jingoistic and sometimes lying low, subdued though not eliminated by a liberal, Western-oriented mood of the moment. We shall review this history of *Nihonjinron* discourse in Chapter Seven.

In examining the history of *Nihonjinron* over the past century and a half, it becomes clear that we have no adequate empirical or quantitative evidence of the extent of its effect on the general populace. In the tradition of intellectual history (*shisō-shi*), one is apt to examine the thoughts of a small number of intellectuals and trace their lineage through other small numbers of scholars who were influenced by them. I have no quarrel with such an endeavor: it has its own methodology, agenda, paradigm, and theoretical framework. It is a self-contained scholarship, more or less, with, of course, relevance to other related phenomena, be they political institutions or economic change. But a question arises in this tradition of examining intellectual history by dealing with great scholars and their thoughts: To what extent do intellectuals' views reflect the thoughts and attitudes of common people, and vice versa? How representative is the sample?

Most historians generally do not address the issue of how pervasively intellectuals' thoughts are accepted among ordinary people because there is no way of fathoming the pervasiveness. My concern is precisely with this issue, though I have to admit that data are lacking. It is because of this lack of data that I concentrate on the modern period, though I will devote Chapter Seven to delving into the *Nihonjinron* of earlier periods.

As an American once wryly remarked, Japanese intellectuals are in some sense leaders without followers: they posit themselves to be different from the masses and win their stake by expressing uncommon views. Though there is some validity in this view, they would have difficulty earning their keep if their treatises did not resonate with a wide audience. For their reputation is established only in part through appraisal of their works by fellow academics and more through their popularity among the general readership of the popular magazines and newspapers for which they write.

Still, there is a problem in establishing how much intellectuals' views are representative of those of the general public. We know little of the common people's thinking in the late Tokugawa and early Meiji eras. In the present era, there are more data on the common people; what is perhaps more important, investigators as their contemporaries have the privilege of being able to intuit, feel, and sense what ideas seem acceptable through their own personal experience in the culture. They can also sense which ideas seem outlandish, a privilege increasingly denied when dealing with a distant past.

Having said this, I must admit that only a blurred line separates 'intellectual history' in the conventional sense of analyzing intellectuals' thoughts from the present endeavor to analyze *Nihonjinron* as the expression of common people's worldview insofar as it is gleaned from *Nihonjinron* writings. No hard-and-fast line will be maintained in this book. As I deal with *Nihonjinron* of the past in later chapters, I will increasingly rely on the writings of a few well-known intellectuals of the time. Nonetheless, our fundamental concern and interest will remain the view of a broad spectrum of the Japanese. It is for this reason that I examine publications of wide popularity rather than sophisticated writings of ivory-tower scholars.

## Anthropological Analysis of *Nihonjinron*

There are four book-length critiques of *Nihonjinron* – by Roy Andrew Miller (1982), Ross Mouer and Yoshio Sugimoto (1986), Peter Dale (1986), and Yoshino Kosaku (1992, 1997). In Miller's and Dale's critiques, and in much of Mouer and Sugimoto's, *Nihonjinron* propositions are taken at face value as purportedly true and valid empirical statements. These critics then demonstrate the invalidity of the statements on methodological, theoretical, or conceptual grounds. Miller and Dale, in particular, endeavor to belittle the whole enterprise of *Nihonjinron*. The volume by Mouer and Sugimoto retains a good deal more balance, although they too at times seem to be more seriously interested in the unworthiness of *Nihonjinron*. Also, as sociologists they (along with Yoshino, another sociologist) take up mainly sociological aspects of *Nihonjinron*, leaving aside others such as language, race, and culture. Yoshino's book, informed by previous works perhaps, is distinctly more analytical and objective, though total objectivity on a subject of this sort is impossible to expect.

Here I try to correct the shortcomings of the preceding works by being more objective in analysis than Miller and Dale, by examining *Nihonjinron* more comprehensively than Mouer and Sugimoto, and by delving into the anthropology of knowledge as a way of understanding this phenomenon. I also use comparative material from other cultures, as Yoshino does, and try to understand *Nihonjinron* as an instantiation of worldwide national and ethnic phenomena, rather than seeing it as unique to Japan.

Almost never has the *Nihonjinron* phenomenon been regarded as a subject matter for anthropological analysis, although it has been widely alluded to in anthropological literature. In analyzing beliefs about ghosts, one might take a positivist-realist position and expend one's energy disproving the existence of ghosts on scientific grounds and disparaging anyone who maintains such a belief. Or one can treat the belief as a social and cultural given rather than as a physical phenomenon, and investigate, for instance, who is more or less likely to believe in ghosts, and where ghosts are said to appear and why, without being judgmental about those who espouse such beliefs. My approach is the latter. A judgmental approach is tempting, and some have succumbed to it, but there is more to be learned from anthropological detachment.

Thus *Nihonjinron* here is considered a cultural phenomenon to be subjected to anthropological analysis, just like shamanism, kinship structure, or ethnicity. In fact, in thinking about *Nihonjinron* as anthropological subject matter, I might use the term *ethnic identity* just as well, an idea Yoshino (1992, 1997) suggests, for my analysis of *Nihonjinron* does share in its conceptual sphere a good deal with the theory of ethnicity. I hope this suggestion will stimulate thought and discussion on the applicability of the theory of ethnicity to *Nihonjinron* and vice versa.

Being a Japanese term, *Nihonjinron* does conjure up a culturally specific concept not shared by any other culture. Thus use of the very term unwittingly reinforces the *Nihonjinron* assertion that Japan is unique and denies the possibility of a comparative treatment of *Nihonjinron*. Putting *Nihonjinron* in the category of ethnicity immediately offers myriad possibilities of analyzing *Nihonjinron* as a phenomenon common to other cultures. Such a discussion would help bring *Nihonjinron* out of the Japanological closet and into the anthropological parlor for general debate with those who are not necessarily interested in Japan but who share a theoretical interest in ethnic and national identity.

It certainly is not too much to ask whether there are phenomena like (not to say identical to) *Nihonjinron* elsewhere around the globe. If we conceptualize *Nihonjinron* as a discourse on national identity, we should find similar or comparable phenomena throughout the world. By examining *Nihonjinron* as a species of cultural nationalism (Befu 1993; Yoshino 1992, 1997), we place Japan in comparative anthropological literature, rather than isolate it as an exceptional or unique species in the anthropological zoo.

In this endeavor, I shall consider how well we can see *Nihonjinron* as a cultural model or a worldview of the sort anthropologists discuss. Since Hobsbawm's work (1983) on 'invention of tradition,' cultural tradition has been interpreted as a result of conscious invention or construction. I shall try to understand *Nihonjinron* in this light.

It is in this spirit of applying anthropological concepts and theories derived from experiences outside Japan that I propose to investigate *Nihonjinron*. At any rate, comparative and theoretical analyses of *Nihonjinron* are rare indeed. Bluntly put, the anthropology of *Nihonjinron* has just begun.

## Continuing Interest

The heyday of current *Nihonjinron* publication was probably in the 1960s through the 1980s, although before and after these dates, one does see important publications on the subject. In terms of the number of monographs published, one sees surging interest in the 1960s, peaking in the 1970s, and somewhat tapering off in the 1980s. This is the reason that most citations in this book come from these decades. One reason why Aoki Tamotsu could write a postwar history of *Nihonjinron* in 1990 is that the surge of interest in the topic had to some extent subsided, allowing him to take stock of the postwar trends.

Yet interest in *Nihonjinron* is scarcely dead; important publications in the field continued to appear through the 1990s as well. Iwanami Shoten, the premier academic publisher, has published a thirteen-volume set on the contemporary *Nihonjinron*, edited by Kawai Hayao and Nakazawa Shin'ichi (1996–1998), covering such topics as the Japanese identity, family and sex, schools, religion, and science. As if this is not enough, Iwanami is also publishing another eleven-volume series edited by Aoki and others (1999) with essentially the same title (*Modern Nihonjinron*).

Single-volume works in *Nihonjinron* also continue to appear. Umehara Takeshi, the founding director-general of the International Center for Japanese Studies and a noted player in *Nihonjinron* game, is the editor of a relatively recent piece (1990) in this genre, which saw its fourteenth printing in 1997. Another recent *Nihonjinron* anthology, questioning whether Japan is homogeneous, was compiled by a former faculty member of the International Center for Japanese Studies, Hamaguchi Eshun (also Esyun)(1996). First published in 1996, it had gone through four printings by 1999. In 1998 he also published another anthology asking 'What is Japanese society?' (Hamaguchi 1998). Noted philosopher Tsurumi Shunsuke (1997) has recently edited a book dealing with 'the heart' of the Japanese, attempting to get at the Japanese psyche through popular culture.

Linking genes to culture, Takeuchi Kumiko's *Nihonjinron* (1999) seeks the origins of Japanese character in a certain virus common in Japan. Amino Yoshihiko (2000) asks, 'What is Japan?' – one of the favorite rhetorical questions in this genre, though his answer comes from the left field, arguing for heterogeneity rather than homogeneity of Japanese culture. Treatises arguing for Japanese-style management, familiar since the 1960s, are still being produced (Itagaki 1997; Kagono 1997). Thus *Nihonjinron* publication is hardly a dying enterprise. It is likely to continue to be a long-run publishing industry in Japan, ebbing and flowing, however, as the geopolitical and geoeconomic tide of Japanese history turns, as discussed in the last chapter of this book.

Given the fact that the day of upsurge in *Nihonjinron* interest has at least temporarily passed – until no doubt the next one comes along – this is a good time to take stock and cogitate on the meaning of *Nihonjinron* as a national pastime, which, as we will see, began two hundred years ago and has persisted through the vicissitudes of history. The content of *Nihonjinron*, its whys and wherefores, can be examined now with relative dispassion and objectivity when we can distance ourselves from the period of frenzied *Nihonjinron* activity.

# 2  The Nature of the Beast

What is unique about Japan, or for that matter, about any culture, may be argued from any number of different points of view – environment, social organization, religion, esthetic value. The *Nihonjinron* advanced by a particular author tends to emphasize a specific approach, be it ecological, psychological, or linguistic, but in totality *Nihonjinron* writings range the gamut of the cultural landscape. Since hundreds of publications deal with this topic, and scores of writers engage in this national pastime, it is not possible to cover the subject matter in these few pages except by summarizing representative arguments. Suffice it for our purposes to sample arguments of a few *Nihonjinron* writers for each of the major approaches.

What follows is a composite picture of *Nihonjinron*, putting together different approaches for a more-or-less comprehensive picture of *Nihonjinron*. I do not imply that different approaches are always consistent with one another. As we shall see in Chapter Seven, diametrically opposite propositions have been advanced by *Nihonjinron* writers at different times in the modern history of Japan. What follows is the *Nihonjinron* as presented in the contemporary Japan of the last three to four decades.

## Yanagita Kunio

Before we even begin to review the contents of *Nihonjinron*, we should acknowledge the enormous debt in this genre to folklorist Yanagita Kunio (1875–1962), whose influence we simply cannot overestimate. Single-handed, he trained scores of folklorists and created a school of Japanese folklore studies with far-reaching consequences. Yanagita and his numerous students investigated and clarified the basic nature of 'the Japanese folk (*jōmin*).' Their contributions range over the whole of Japanese cultural practices from folk beliefs, rituals and festivals, and ancestral rites to basic values, rural community structure, gender, and the kinship system.

This huge reservoir of knowledge about Japanese folk practices has provided the ingredients for constructing *Nihonjinron* for many of its writers. Many of Yanagita's followers, in fact, became important players in this genre. In 1954 Yanagita himself edited a volume titled *Nihonjin* (Yanagita 1954), in which he and his students, Wakamori Tarō, Hori Ichirō, and others, contributed chapters on Japaneseness, folk beliefs of the Japanese, the Japanese conception of authority, and other topics.

## Ecology

The view that Japan is a resource-poor nation with frequent natural calamities – typhoons, droughts, floods, landslides, earthquakes, and so on – has been popular for many generations. What is important in this argument is not simply Japan's physical geography, but the supposedly inextricable relationship between that geography and the cultural life of the Japanese (Chiba ed. 1980; Misawa 1979; Miyamoto 1967; Sabata 1974; Sekiguchi 1983; H. Suzuki 1975; Yamada 1978). This view was perhaps most systematically propounded by Watsuji Tetsurō in his *Fūdo*. Although it was first published in 1935, I take up this book in discussing the contemporary version of ecological *Nihonjinron* because it is still regularly being reprinted – on the average of once a year – to meet continued demand and because it is one of the most referenced works in *Nihonjinron*. It was translated in 1961 as *A Climate* – though 'Climate and Culture,' as originally proposed by Watsuji himself and as the later edition (1988) came to be titled, would have been a much more appropriate English title. The book is not so much concerned with the supposed effect of weather as such upon Japanese culture as with what Augustin Berque has called 'mediance' (1988) – that is, the relationship between environment and culture.

In this classic, Watsuji classifies Eurasia into three ecological types: monsoon, desert, and pastoral. Japan is in the monsoon belt that stretches off the east coast of the Asiatic continent. To distinguish Japan from other monsoon cultures, Watsuji notes that Japan is also exposed to the severe climatic effect of the Arctic air coming down from the north. From this combination of warm and wet air from the south and bitter cold Arctic wind blown across

Siberia and the Japan Sea onto Japan, Watsuji derives everything that uniquely characterizes Japan – from Japan's wet rice cultivation and family structure to its national character, ethos, and esthetics. According to Watsuji, the open architecture of Japanese homes, which are adapted to humidity and heat, was necessitated by the monsoon climate. This open style of architecture in turn relates to the absence of privacy in Japan and even to the denial of individual rights and promotion of collective orientation.

Watsuji's theory about climate and culture has had a far-reaching effect on generations of scholars writing in the *Nihonjinron* genre. For example, Chikamatsu (1978), Kimata (1978), and Tsukiyama (1972) basically accepted Watsuji's position and elaborated his views in their own works. Kōyama Iwao (1941: 202), like Watsuji, derives Japanese sensitivity toward nature from the physical conditions of Japan. For him the small size of the island country is responsible for the Japanese love of miniature and miniaturization, such as the seventeen-syllable *haiku* and the thirty-one-syllable *tanka* poetry, rather than epic poems, and has created the art of *bonsai*, affording planting-pot size landscape.[3] Corporate groups, such as peasant communities, also developed in rural Japan because of the closed nature of the village environment induced by wet rice cultivation, according to these and other ecologically oriented *Nihonjinron* writers.

Kōyama (1941) also derives from environmental factors Japanese optimism, this-worldly character, fusion of art and life, and even patriotism. Psychologist Miyagi Otoya (1972), starting from the same assumption of the harsh, destructive environment of Japan, derives certain personality types among the Japanese. These ideas will be taken up later, in the section on psychological components of *Nihonjinron*. But it is noteworthy that Miyagi contrasts Japan with the West, saying that Japan did not try to 'conquer nature' as the West did, which he regards as a manifestation of sadism, but instead merely tried to 'adapt to it,' which to him is a manifestation of masochism. Later, however, Miyagi (1976) tempers this direct environment-to-personality argument by noting that personality, though derived from environment, is mediated through living patterns ('food, shelter, and clothing').

This approach, which emphasizes negative aspects of ecological conditions, such as the smallness of the island nation and the cold and harsh climate in which Japan finds itself, should be contrasted with the approach in *Nihonjinron* that sees the environment as basically benign. For example, Chikamatsu (1978) characterizes Japan's climate as being 'mild (*on'wa*),' 'subtle (*bimyō*),' and 'delicate (*sensai*).' To him, this sense of nature in turn creates a unique literary esthetic, as especially seen in *haiku* poetry, with its distinct sense of seasonality.

## Subsistence Economy

That wet rice cultivation necessitated formation of village corporacy is an argument maintained by many writers and is generally accepted as a truism by such *Nihonjinron* writers as Sabata (1972), Tamaki (1978), and Tsukuba (1969). The need for cooperation in maintaining an irrigation system and in rice transplanting, harvesting, and other agricultural activities in ancient Japan is supposed to have created a tightly knit, perhaps even oppressively tyrannical corporate community that demands conformity, consensus, and cooperation and does not allow members to express individuality and assert their rights (Tamaki 1978).

Arguments in this respect are often made by explicitly comparing Japan with 'the West,' where in one type of argument, a pastoral economy is supposed to have prevailed in the distant past. In pastoralism, the argument goes, what is important is the individual ownership of the herd and the grazing land. This requirement impeded formation of an oppressive corporate community and even corporate family, as wet rice cultivation supposedly required. The same force of wet rice cultivation requiring corporate effort, it is argued, has also created *amae* – the Japanese propensity for psychological interdependence – and the fundamental, closely knit kinship units of Japan (Sabata 1964: 134).

According to the late Ishida Eiichirō, a leading anthropologist of the past generation, the pastoral economy of Europe is responsible for the monotheism expressed not only in Christianity but also in Judaism and Islam, all of which arose in a pastoral context. This religious base has much to do with the nature of European civilization and the 'core personality' of Europeans (Ishida 1969: 179–183). He contrasts Japan with Europe in these respects, drawing on Watsuji's ideas and pointing out Japan's animistic religion and other characteristics of Japanese culture (1969: 150–152). Araki (1973) and Iwasaki (1980) similarly contrast the Japanese agrarian economy with the Western pastoral economy, deriving from that contrast the basis of Japanese group orientation and Western individualism.

## Social Structure

To those discussing what they see as the peculiarly Japanese social structure, no feature is more salient than the idea of group orientation, or *groupism*. Using this feature, scholars have sought to analyze not only the family (Kawashima 1957) but also the master-disciple relationship in traditional arts and crafts and, above all, the Japanese company organization. It is not far from the mark to say that most American social scientists concerned with Japan's social structure and the behavior of the Japanese, myself most certainly included, have at one time or another endorsed this model.

For example, historian Edwin Reischauer espoused this group model half a century ago in *The United States and Japan* (1950). Nobutaka Ike (1978), a political scientist, has argued that an understanding of the group-oriented behavior of the Japanese is central to understanding political processes in Japan. This view also dominates the more popular coverage of Japan and the Japanese in the United States. *Growing Up Japanese* – a film produced by the United States–Japan Trade Council – and *The Japanese* – a National Broadcasting Company 'documentary' – both stress the idea that group orientation is the most salient feature of Japanese society. The concept of 'Japan, Inc.,' made popular decades ago by Herman Kahn (1970), is an extension of the model, one that treats Japanese society as a monolithic entity.

This wide acceptance of the groupist notion of Japan in the West in turn has caused many Japanese *Nihonjinron* writers to take groupism as the centerpiece of their own *Nihonjinron* and to write extensively on this theme. The Japanese are wont to be uncritically accepting of Westerners' ideas – for reasons to be explicated later.

The Japanese term *sūdan shugi*, a translation of *groupism*, has a more neutral or even positive connotation than the English term itself, which sounds somewhat flippant. Its value index is definitely lower than that of *individualism* and its cognates in other European languages. This connotative difference unfortunately immediately gives Westerners the feeling that the social ideology of the Japanese is something to look down upon. When expressed in Japanese the term is at least coeval with – or if anything has a higher value index than – 'individualism (*kojin shugi*),' which in Japanese strongly implies selfishness or egotism at the expense of others. One should not be so ethnocentric as to be guided by the connotation of the English term in evaluating this matter.

Deriving this group orientation from the environment or a subsistence economy (Iwasaki 1980: 34–35; Kenmochi 1978; Tsukiyama 1972: 27) and from rural origins (Tamaki 1978: 202–207) is a popular exercise among *Nihonjinron* writers. Kenmochi, for example, considers intensive wet rice cultivation as responsible for Japan's groupism (1978: 173). Watsuji does not go so far as to derive (in a causal sense) the corporate community from wet rice cultivation, but he considers the Japanese kinship system called *ie* (family) as 'monsoonish.' For Watsuji, the most important feature of *ie* is its totality, or corporacy (*zentaisei*), which is represented by the head of *ie* (1935: 147–148). 'The Japanese throughout their history have aimed to suppress their egotism for family relations,' according to Watsuji (p. 142). Watsuji then relates *ie* to the state, equating filial piety in *ie* to loyalty for the state, regarding the state to be the ultimate ('highest level') totality while the *ie* is the immediate ('lowest level') totality (p. 148). Watsuji affirms loyalty to the state and also to the emperor as the representative of the state.

Other Japanese writers have thus written to argue for the group orientation of the Japanese without necessarily deriving it from rural background (for example, Inuta 1977; Kawamoto 1990; Maniwa 1990). Nakane Chie among them is most prominently known not only in Japan through her best-seller in Japanese (1967), but also outside Japan through her *Japanese Society* (1970). Nakane is explicit about the defining criteria of the Japanese group: (1) the notion of 'frame,' which she defines as 'a criterion that sets a boundary and gives a common basis to a set of individuals who are allocated to or involved in it' (1970: 1), (2) the predominance of vertical relationships, (3) exclusivity of membership, that is, one belongs to one and only one group, and (4) hostility toward outsiders.

Nakane's model of Japanese society has won wide acceptance among the Japanese. Aida Yūji, himself a well-known *Nihonjinron* writer, has fully embraced the notion of Japan as a 'vertical society' (1976, 1980). Inuta (1977) contrasts what he calls the 'C' type society with the 'D' type society; the former is group oriented and the latter, individualistic. The latter emphasizes individual rights, duties, and conscience, whereas in the former these characteristics are absent. Thus in Japan, members of a group constantly 'impose' upon each other. This is part of being a member of a 'destiny-sharing corporate community (*ummei kyōdōtai*).'

The group model of Japanese society is based on the idea of a hierarchically organized group. The paternalistic leader at the apex serves to satisfy both the affective and the instrumental needs of the organization's members. The psychological process of emotional dependence supporting this structure has been referred to as *amae* (Doi 1971, 1973). Generally speaking, those in lower social positions seek emotional satisfaction by prevailing and depending upon their social superiors, although reversed dependence (of a superior on subordinates) is also an essential process. The hierarchical and affective features of *amae* are etiologically those seen in the mother-child relationship, which is believed to be at the core of the socialization process. Normatively, instrumental and expressive provision supplied by a superior for subordinates is summarized in the concept of 'indebtedness (*on*).' This concept implies a normative obligation known as *giri*, a moral imperative that one should repay one's debt. For the subordinate, this is done · through giving loyal service to the superior.

In the group model, harmony through cooperation and conformity among group members are prime virtues; conversely, open conflict and competition are taboo. Because they reduce the level of mutual affective satisfaction among members, those who are competitive or conflict-oriented are sanctioned in various ways such as being ostracized (Smith 1961) or shamed (Benedict 1946). Emphasis on harmonious interpersonal relationships goes hand in hand with the norms found in ritualized, formal behavioral patterns, which tend to reduce, if not totally eliminate, open conflict or embarrassment.

As an ideal type, the group is structured so that all members are selflessly oriented toward the goals of the group. With benevolence and magnanimity, the leader helps, supports, and protects his followers at all times regardless of personal cost. In return, subordinate members are expected to express their uncalculating loyalty and devotion.[4]

Sociologist Hamaguchi Eshun's conception of the Japanese group begins with the notion of 'contextualism (*kanjin shugi or aidagara shugi*),' emphasizing the total situation in which an individual is placed as the basic unit of society rather than the individual stripped to himself or herself (Hamaguchi 1977).[5] Hamaguchi argues that previous understanding of Japanese society has been marred by 'methodological individualism,' which developed through Western experience. He argues it applies to Western society but not to Japan, for which a different and new methodological assumption is needed. This is what he calls 'methodological contextualism.'

Hamaguchi distinguishes between 'groupism' (*sūdan shugi*), which to him is a concept deriving from Western culture, and 'corporativism' (*kyōdō dantai shugi*), which is uniquely Japanese. Groupism, according to him, pits the individual against the group and places priority on the group. In this sense, individualism and groupism are antithetical and contradictory concepts. According to Hamaguchi, the Japanese individual sees the self to be unified (*ittaika*) with the group, meaning that through achieving the goal of the group, individual members achieve their own goals, contrary to the Western sense in which the group and the individual are at odds with one another.

Some critics disagree with Nakane on the characterization of the Japanese group, arguing for the importance of horizontal ties – relationships among equals in an organization – rather than vertical ties. Tsuda, for example, argues this point with respect to business organizations, saying that vertical emphasis is rather a European characteristic (1977: 261). Yoneyama also (1976) has called attention to the importance of collegiality in Japanese society.

## Japanese Management

As whys and wherefores of Japan's rapid economic growth and the success of the Japanese economy in the international scene became an academic topic, literally scores of books have been published in the field of 'Japanese-style management.' 'The Japanese economic miracle' is attributed at least in part to this peculiar management style, which in turn derives from more generalized Japanese organizational principles based on group orientation. Many emphasize the importance of groupist paternalism in Japan's economic enterprises, where management supposedly looks after employees with benevolence, providing fringe benefits and guaranteeing permanent employment. Through such practices, it has been posited, employers are able to claim the devotion and loyalty of their employees.

The three major organizational pillars upholding the Japanese firm are said to be permanent employment, seniority, and enterprise unionism, commonly referred to as 'the three sacred treasures' of Japanese management. Underlying these pillars are elements of Japanese group orientation such as communitarianism, treatment of members as whole persons, mutual trust, emphasis on harmony, and the like.

Abegglen (1958) was one of the first scholars to recognize the connection between Japan's organizational style and its economic success. Since then Ballon (1968), Brown (1966), Rohlen (1974), and numerous others in the West have supported essentially the same thesis. What is important for our discussion of cultural identity of the Japanese is that these discussions are not conducted only by foreigners awed by Japanese economic accomplishments: the same argument is carried on by Japanese themselves. Indeed a recent *Books in Print* (Nihon Shoseki Shuppan Kyōkai 2000) lists as many as thirty-four titles that begin with the phrase *Nihon-teki keiei* (Japanese-style management). Some of the recognized authorities in this field are Gotō (1983), Hazama (1971), Iwata (1978), Nishida Kōzō (1978), Odaka (1981, 1984), and Tsuda (1977). Let us briefly review their views on Japanese-style management.[6]

Gotō Tetsuhiko (1983), a graduate in economics of Keiō University and author of a number of books on management, is perhaps more explicit than any of the others in deriving the Japanese management system from the tenets of *Nihonjinron*. He begins his analysis by invoking the concept of *yūgen*, which is probably about as ineffable and purely Japanese as any concept expressing Japanese ethos and esthetics. Cultural values are ultimately the basic motive force, according to Gotō. Like Watsuji, he starts with the premise that monsoon ecology provided the setting for wet rice cultivation, which in turn was responsible for the Japanese corporate rural community, in short, groupism (1983: 250). According to him, personality traits of hard work, perseverance, and industry – along with esthetic qualities like *wabi* (subdued simplicity) – can also be accounted for by this ecology. This rural background then defines for Gotō the Japanese-style agrarian-type management (*nōkō minzoku gata keiei*). Devotion to the group, priority of the group over the individual, and emphasis on harmony within the group are all derived from Japanese spiritualism (*Nihon seishin shugi*). To Gotō, this groupism is also responsible for the excesses of Japan's nationalism, the violence of the Japanese imperial army and the Red Army of the postwar era, and even the hot-rod riders called *bōsōzoku*.

Another important basis of the Japanese management system is said to be the societal and cultural homogeneity and monolinguality, which allow strong cooperation and effective nonverbal communication. Gotō regards various company benefits, such as company housing, family allowance, health plans, transportation subsidies, expense accounts, and pensions as constituting *on*, a debt to be returned to the employer in the form of loyalty to the company (1983: 26). He also emphasizes the importance of empathy (*jō no bunka*), which allows functionally diffuse relationships and 'generalized exchange among employees.'

Urabe (1978), another management specialist, also derives the 'three sacred treasures' of the Japanese management system from Japan's traditional past. Management through respect for the total personality of the individual (*makoto gokoro*) is to him the basis of the Japanese system (1978: 188).

Tsuda, a management specialist at Hitotsubashi University – the preeminent institution for economics and business management – argues that what he calls 'the corporate livelihood community (*kyōdō seikatsutai*)' was born of wet rice cultivation, and uses it as the starting point of his theory of the Japanese group. Tsuda further argues that principles governing *ie* (family) also govern the Japanese group. *Ie* as a quasi-kinship concept emphasizes unigeniture, with the consequent hierarchy of siblings and use of adoption for continuation of the organization (*ie*). Historically, this system has created a business organization based on the *ie* principle. This agrarian social structure of *ie* presumably has been transferred to industrial organization (Tsuda 1977, 1982), as well as to the urban setting (Tamaki 1978: 197, 204–207).

Tsuda regards the company as a 'corporate livelihood community' where 'members express their desire to be loved, to be intimate with others, to respect others, and to fulfill' their egos (1977: 248). This sounds much like Doi's *amae*, even though Tsuda emphatically denies the need for concepts like *amae* to talk about management systems.

According to Odaka Kunio (1981), an erstwhile dean of industrial sociology who taught at Tokyo University, Japanese groupism is derived from the following four factors: (1) wet rice cultivation; (2) the *ie*-based household system in which membership was not limited to kinship base and which was organized into a main and branch (*honke-bunke*) family system, making up a corporate group of households; (3) the feudal (*daimyō*) domain (*han*) of the Tokugawa period (1603–1868) as the largest collective unit of households, constituting a political community; and (4) pantheism, which allowed each corporate community to have its own guardian deity. Odaka, like many others, calls this 'a destiny-sharing corporate community (*ummei kyōdōtai*)' and regards it as the basis of company organization (1981: 55–79).

Odaka argues that the Japanese management system is predicated upon the premise that the worker will participate in the company enterprise as a whole individual, rather than in a limited capacity, simply 'selling' specific skills to the company. Odaka identifies two basic principles: priority of the totality over the individual member, and workers' cooperative efforts to reach goals. He also identifies seven specific characteristics of the Japanese management system (1981: 34–43):

- Authoritarian management
- Group decision making and group responsibility
- Emphasis on harmony and effort
- Seniority
- Permanent employment
- Affective relationships
- Enterprise unionism.

Many of these – especially emphasis on the group, harmony in interpersonal relations, and affectionalism – are by now familiar to the reader as hallmarks of *Nihonjinron*. Further, the notion of 'seniority' echoes the 'verticality principle' of Nakane's well-known thesis, while permanent employment is seen as a consequence of groupism.

Nishida Kōzō, another management specialist, invokes the concept of 'unified cohesion (*ittaika ketsugō*).' According to him, the Japanese group concept has three elements: (1) assumption of uniform nature of human beings, closely related to the notion of cultural and ethnic homogeneity (1978: 89–90, 40–48); (2) identity with one's group; and (3) priority of the group over the individual.

Nishida, too, sees groupism as a managerial ideology. He derives special characteristics of Japanese management from the characteristics noted thus far. For Nishida, a Japanese enterprise is constituted on the principle of mutual identification between the firm and its employees and among employees – between a manager and subordinates within a subunit, and between subunits of a firm (1978: 117–125). This mutual identification, according to Nishida, takes place horizontally as well as vertically. He thus casts doubt on Nakane's model of Japanese society, which emphasizes verticality at the expense of egalitarian bonds. Nishida argues that postwar groupism differs from its predecessor. Before and during the war, groupism demanded that members sacrifice themselves for the good of the group. In the postwar version, incursion of individualism from the West has caused members to think about their own interest and welfare and to serve their group only insofar as the group serves their individual purposes. Nishida calls this latter type 'instrumental groupism' (1978: 288). He regards the Japanese management system as superior to Western system in certain respects, but he also admits certain problems attendant on the system (1978: chaps. 6, 7).

Hazama's affiliation to the groupist *Nihonjinron* theme is evident in his 1971 book on Japanese-style management, which is subtitled 'Merits and Demerits of Groupism (*Shūdan shugi no kōzai*).' Hazama accepts the observations of such Westerners as London *Economist* reporters Abbeglen and Vogel regarding Japanese groupism and considers it the basic building block of the Japanese management system. His emphasis on group harmony, reciprocal favors among members, categorical distinctions between members and outsiders, preference for functionally diffuse relationships between supervisor and subordinates, and efficacy of nonverbal communication all hark back to the groupist thesis of *Nihonjinron*. Hazama derives the Japanese managerial welfarism of the postwar years historically from what he calls the managerial familism of the prewar days.

The Nippon Steel Corporation, the largest steel manufacturer in Japan, has published a handbook called *Nippon: The Land and Its People* (Shin Nihon Seitetsu Kōhō Kikaku-Shitsu ed. 1984) primarily to provide employees assigned to foreign posts with information about Japan that they may not know, and as a guide for them to inform foreigners about Japan in case they are asked. The book is widely marketed in ordinary bookstores, as well, and other major Japanese multinationals have followed suit and published similar books. The Nippon Steel book has gone through many editions and many printings. It has been divided into two volumes, one on culture and tradition and the other on con-temporary society (Shin Nihon Seitetsu Kōhō Kikaku-Shitsu ed. 1992a, 1992b), and now covers a wide range of topics from geography and history through politics and economics to society and culture. These issues conveniently interface pages in Japanese with pages of English translation. Here is a book that was designed to foster a certain image of Japan to its sponsor's employees and to publicize that image to foreigners. It is instructive to go through it to see what sorts of image of Japan Nippon Steel wishes to propagate. Prominent in this image is the Japanese group orientation. In the section on the group affiliation of the Japanese it says:

> The wet-paddy rice cultivation method used in Japan made it necessary to work in groups and have a system of joint cooperation. The people in an area had to band together during the regular periods of intensive work involved in the planting and harvesting of the rice, and it was also necessary for these groups to institute some system among themselves for allocating the water for the paddies. All this instilled in the agricultural workers a consciousness of belonging to their localized farming communities.
>
> Also, with the spread of the Confucian ethic from China there was a strengthening of the concept of belonging to a family group, and, among the warrior class, of belonging to a clan.

Against this historical background, the modern employee's sense of belonging to his company is further strengthened by the systems of lifetime employment, ranking according to the number of years of service, and internal welfare schemes, which are features of company management in Japan (1984: 327–329).

I have taken extra space here to go into the details of the special application of the groupist aspect of *Nihonjinron* to Japanese management because of its importance in the popular discussion of Japanese-style management, and above all, in explaining Japan's economic success in cultural terms. It should be clear from this discussion that groupism is a central concept not only in *Nihonjinron* but also in the theory of Japanese management.

## Psychology

Earlier *Nihonjinron* writers of an ecological persuasion, such as Watsuji, considered environment to be an important part of the psychological makeup of the Japanese. Watsuji maintains that the monsoon climate gives Japanese both receptivity (*juyōsei*) and perseverance. Receptivity means for Watsuji emotional fulfillment and at the same time quiet endurance. Just as a typhoon happens suddenly, this emotion, too, is capable of sudden shifts and changes in short spurts (Watsuji 1935: 134–138).

As we saw earlier, Miyagi Otoya (1969, 1976), a prominent psychologist of the past generation and perhaps a rear guard of the old ecological school, basically accepts the causal priority of the environment in determining the personality of the Japanese mediated by the intervening variables of food, shelter, and clothing. According to Miyagi, there are two major personality types represented in Japan: the manic-depressive type, distributed in southwestern Japan, and the schizophrenic type, found in northeastern Japan. These two are archaic types going back to prehistoric times, whose remnants one can still see among contemporary Japanese. For Miyagi, the Japanese living in the prehistoric Jōmon period (12,000 B.P. to 2300 B.P.) were schizophrenic; the manic-depressive type, with its rice-growing technology and attendant culture, moved into Japan from the Asiatic continent in the following Yayoi period (2300 B.P. to 1700 B.P.). According to Miyagi, when these two traits mixed through intermarriage, the result was to create an unyielding spirit (*kachiki*). This temperament makes the Japanese both proud and vain. It makes them haughty to the weaker but subservient to the stronger. The same temperament makes the Japanese conformists, and the propensity to conform makes them imitate others. This unyielding spirit, strangely, also allows them to change their mind 180 degrees without feeling bad, as happened at the end of World War II, when Japanese all became converted from emperor worshipers to democracy worshipers. Miyagi also derives from the same sources a host of other personality traits for Japanese, such as neurosis, hypersensitivity, excitability, and readiness to blame others.

Egami Namio (1967, 1985, 1986) marshals forth his well-known horseback rider hypothesis on the origins of the Japanese nation to derive Japanese personality. In brief, Egami proposes that horseback riders of Inner Asia invaded Japan from the end of the fourth century to the fifth century and politically unified Japan, providing an overlay of pastoral culture on the agrarian base. This explains, to his satisfaction at any rate, the supposed dual characteristics of the Japanese, who are on one hand tractable, conservative, fatalistic, and authoritarian – traits deriving from their agrarian origins – and on the other hand curious, progressive, open, utilitarian, and pragmatic – traits representing their pastoral background (1985: 96–98).

Doi Takeo (1971), Kawai Hayao (1984), Minami Hiroshi (1954), and Okonogi Keigo (1982) are perhaps among the best-known professional psychologists writing in the *Nihonjinron* vein. Minami's earlier work (1954) characterized Japanese personality largely in terms of such qualities as sadness, melancholy, fatalism, unhappiness, and loneliness. But one must see this assortment of negative personality traits, as we shall in Chapter Seven, in the context of the postwar ethos where Japanese were going through a period of remorse, confessing to the guilt of the war and blaming themselves for their misfortune in a war-ravaged country.

Doi (1971) has built a whole theory of the Japanese national character on the basis of the one concept of *amae*, which identifies the signal Japanese trait denoting mutual psychological dependency of primary group members, starting in the family with a child depending on parents, but later extending this dependency to significant others in other social groups. For Doi, this unique concept becomes the basis of the personality makeup of the Japanese.[7] A similar view has been expressed by Kimura (1972).

During socialization, Doi's reasoning goes, a close emotional bond develops between mother and child through various mechanisms that need not detain us here. Dependence is encouraged rather than discouraged in Japan – in contrast with the situation in North America, where encouragement of social and emotional independence is the guiding normative value. Accordingly, adult Japanese continue to seek emotional security, in and outside the family: in school from their teachers and at work from their superior. Since mother is seen as a source of nurturance as well as of psychic security, those in a superior position fulfill the mother's role outside the family; they provide satisfaction both for instrumental and expressive needs of others, so the argument goes.

This notion of mutual dependency corroborates with Hamaguchi's (1977) and Minami's social psychological approaches, in which members of Japanese society are said to be bound to one another through mutual trust and obligation. Minami's basic approach in his later work (1983) is that the Japanese lack self-conception and self-identity, which in turn brings about dependence on others and on the group to which they belong.

Okonogi has developed the concept of the 'Ajase complex' (1982), which contrasts with the Western Oedipus complex, the Freudian foundation of the Western personality. Unlike the Oedipus complex, in which sexuality is the central theme, in the Ajase complex mutual love and the son's longing for the mother are the focal notions, along with – though too complex to develop here – a contradictory notions of unity, reciprocity (or mutuality), resentment, masochism, forgiveness, and a sense of guilt between mother and child.

## Ethos

The unique geist of the Japanese is argued in innumerable treatises, perhaps the abstract, speculative nature of the concept encouraging all to join the bandwagon. This geist is often expressed in such Japanese terms as *Yamato damashii* (spirit of Japan) (Saitō 1972,

1980; Tanikawa 1947: 133–174), *kokoro* ('the heart' of Japan or the Japanese) (Tanikawa 1940, 1947; Sera 1965), and *Nihon seishin* (Japanese spirit) (Aizawa 1976).

Let us take *kokoro* as an example par excellence of the Japanese ethos. There are several books with the identical title of *Nihon no Kokoro* – 'The Heart of Japan' (Ishigami 1969, 1971; Itsui 1973; Makino ed. 1995, 1996; Maruyama 1991; Shin Nihon Seitetsu Kōhō Kikaku-Shitsu ed. 1987, 1992a, 1992b). There are also several more books entitled *Nihonjin no Kokoro* – 'The Heart of the Japanese.' (Itsuki et al. 1992; Tsurumi ed. 1997; Umesao et al. eds. 1974; Wakamori 1981; Yoshida 1996). Here 'heart' is obviously used metaphorically, as one might in the expression 'the heart of America' or 'of Russia,' with the focus on fondness and senti-mentality, spiritual and emotional overtones distilling the spirit of Japanese culture. Regardless of the contents of such books, it is important that they bear a title that symbolizes the essence of Japan.

These books bearing the term *kokoro* in the title discuss notable personalities in Japanese history. Presumably these individuals embody the essence or the 'heart' of Japan. In these books, the authors, without explicating the geist presumably found in these personalities, intend for the reader to read between the lines to fathom the subtext on the 'heart' of Japan. For example, Karaki Junzō, author of some twenty books on Japanese literature, literary figures, and other topics, authored *Nihonjin no Kokoro* (1965), which in less than three months went through five printings, in spite of its relative expense – 620 yen – at a time when an ordinary paperback book could be had for about 200 yen. In this book Karaki discusses such notable figures as Matsuo Bashō, arguably the foremost *haiku* poet of all time in Japan; Buddhist priest Ippen; Watsuji Tetsurō, whose effects on *Nihonjinron* through his ecological theory of Japanese culture we have reviewed; Nishida Kitarō, Japan's foremost modern philosopher; Tanabe Hajime, another well-known philosopher; Suzuki Daisetz, who is re-sponsible for disseminating Zen philosophy in the West more than any other single person; Mori Ōgai and Natsume Sōseki, 'naturalist' novelists of the Meiji period; and others.

Like Karaki, Goi, founder of a little-known postwar religious sect called Byakko Shinkōkai, also takes up famous historic figures in his *Nihon no Kokoro* (1973). He elaborates on Saigō Takamori, a much-revered tragic hero who rebelled against the Meiji government and ultimately committed suicide when his army was vanquished by government troops; Yoshida Shōin, one of the foremost ideologues of the 'National Learning' school of the Tokugawa period; Prince Shōtoku, who laid the foundation of the political ideology of Japan back in the seventh century; the aforementioned Matsuo Bashō; Emperor Hirohito; and other notables. Goi, too, leaves it up to the reader to decide what is 'Japanese' about these individuals.

In yet another book of the same title, Yasuda Yojūrō and Nakagawa Kōichi (1969) discuss such well-known figures as Fujita Tsugushi, a modern Western-style painter who worked in Paris most of his life; Sesshū, a Zen priest and painter; Izumi Shikibu, a female poet of the Heian period, active around 1000 C.E.; and others. This methodology of nonmethodology is also pursued in many other treatises of *Nihonjinron*.

Even though these authors and compilers of accounts of notable figures in Japanese history do not tell us why they selected the chosen figures or what about them qualifies as manifesting 'the heart of Japan' or 'the heart of the Japanese,' the term *kokoro* still resonates among Japanese readers. It points to the locus and the substance of quintessential 'Japanliness' – the crux of Japanese culture. It is for this very reason that so many books refer to *kokoro*, which conjures up the essence of the culture and satisfies the nostalgic and primordial feeling of the now modernized, urbanized Japanese living in a technologized, internationalized, and globalized world. Here writers and publishers are well aware of the sales value of titles that refer to the heart of Japan, though they may not be able to spell out what constitutes Japanliness.

Though not bearing the term *kokoro* in the title, Uchimura Kanzō's classic compendium of 'representative Japanese,' published in 1908, follows the same method of recounting famous personages in history (Uchimura 1908b, 1941). Recently Sakata Makoto (1999) has compiled a set 'new representative Japanese,' replacing old guard personalities with new ones from more recent history, such as poet Yosano Akiko, rebel Kōtoku Shūsui, and industrialist Honda Sōichirō.

## Esthetic and Literary Concepts

Japanese cultural philosophers have explicated at length on such esthetic concepts as *ki, iki, wabi, sabi,* and *mono no aware* as keys to understanding Japanese culture. Briefly, *iki* refers to chicness as expressed quintessentially by townspeople of the Tokugawa period – subtle but flashy, subdued but flamboyant at the same time. *Wabi* and *sabi* denote the refined simplicity of quasi-rusticity.[8] *Mono no aware* has to do with melancholic attitudes toward nature and life.

*Iki* as an esthetic concept has been made well known through Kuki's work (1930). *Iki* developed among town merchants in opposition to the esthetics of the ruling samurai, which emphasized asceticism, simplicity, subdued beauty, and the like. *Iki*, on the other hand, is an esthetic quality that developed out of male-female tension without implying a romantic relationship. Iki implies sexual tension, such as that between the worldly women in an entertainment quarter and the men who frequent them. It is a relationship of having fun but not falling in love. A merchant-class man of *iki* in the Tokugawa period enjoyed a certain kind of respect and envy.

Although Kuki's book itself is not within the popular *Nihonjinron* genre, it has been interpreted into more popular vernacular by a number of writers (such as Fukakusa 1971: 184–194; Terai Minako 1979: 214–217). Fukasaku, for example, devotes a section of his *Nihonjinron* treatise (1971: 184–194) to discussing Kuki's theory. Terai (1979), a member of Shisō no Kagaku, a nonacademic group that discusses attitudes, thoughts, and social issues of common people, writes of the esthetics of kimono. In this writing she argues that the beauty of kimono is not in the material clothing itself, but in the wearing of it. Kuki's concept of *iki* comes alive, according to her, in the act of wearing and displaying kimono.

## Language

The view that language contains the secret of the speaker's worldview, thought processes, and the like is an old one. It has been some half a century since Edward Sapir (1949) and Benjamin Whorf (1956) made the idea well known in anthropological circles. Japanese

*Nihonjinron* protagonists may never heard of Sapir or Whorf, but they have taken a position akin to their American counterparts – intellectual forebears of linguistic *Nihonjinron* writers.

The importance of language for ethnic identity has been argued by myriad linguists of all kinds, anthropological, psychological, sociological, as well as practitioners of nationalistic and ethnic movements without technical training in linguistics. *Nihonjinron* claims in this regard are thus only another example, nothing unique. As we have seen, since so much of what is considered Japanese uniqueness derives from concepts expressed in Japanese words that are difficult to translate, language is inevitably at the core of *Nihonjinron*, and it relates to everything from social structure and personality to ethos and esthetics. Thus the relevance of language has already been implied in all the specific Japanese terms introduced. What fuels the fire of the linguistic uniqueness argument is that the Japanese language is natively spoken only by Japanese in Japan and that all Japanese in Japan speak it natively. This one-to-one correspondence, to be discussed further in Chapter Four, enables advocates of *Nihonjinron* to exploit the language to the maximum (Kakehi 1984; Nakamura 1948–49).

Kindaichi Haruhiko (1957, 1975, 1977, 1991), a well-known linguist and son of another well-known linguist (Kyōsuke), has contributed much to linguistic *Nihonjinron*, suggesting that Japanese is an isolated language, meaning it is not related to any other language.[9] He cites an endless controversy about which, if any, of the many disparate and unrelated languages and language groups (including Ainu, Korean, Tibeto-Burmese, Ural-Altaic, and Malayo-Polynesian) might be a cognate language of Japanese. Lack of consensus, he says, is a telltale sign of the Japanese language's lack of affiliation and of its isolation, making Japanese a unique language (1957: 10–12).

Since, in addition, there is supposedly a perfect isomorphism between speakers of the Japanese language and bearers of the Japanese culture, whatever is unique about the language is also unique to the people and culture. This may be contrasted with the situation with English, for example, which is spoken natively by many peoples of recognizably different national and cultural groups. In a situation of this sort, one cannot extract from the language any cultural characteristics unique to its speakers.

Linguistic determinism of the uniqueness of the Japanese culture has been given a 'scientific' validation by one Tsunoda Tadanobu (1978), a medical doctor who found differences in the hemispheric functions of speech between native speakers of Japanese and native speakers of Western languages. According to Tsunoda, European speakers process independent vowels in the right hemisphere along with nonlinguistic sounds such as those of machines, nature, and emotions; in contrast, the Japanese process both independent vowels and nonlinguistic sounds – except those of machines and musical instruments – in the left hemisphere. Since the left hemisphere performs logical and mathematical functions as well, in the Japanese brain, 'logos' and 'pathos' are, as it were, integrated, in contradistinction to the European thought process, where logic and emotion are contrasted or opposed.

Tsunoda's view has received wide publicity, as one would imagine, and for some it has given a stamp of scientific validation for the so far fuzzy, social-science and humanistic – that is, 'impressionistic' – *Nihonjinron* arguments. Tsunoda's view, however, is not entirely accepted by the medical community because of the smallness of the sample and the substandard scientific procedure employed in the study.

The claim of the uniqueness of Japanese culture as derived from language has several aspects, which are discussed in subsequent paragraphs.

**Thought Processes**

That language expresses thought is perhaps a truism with a universal validity. Nakamura Hajime (1948–49) has presented probably the most thorough and systematic argument, treating thought processes among Indians, Chinese, Tibetans, and Japanese, using language as the primary window from which to view the relationship between language and thought. Though his argument is at the scholarly extreme of the scholarly-popular continuum of *Nihonjinron* literature his work has been influential for *Nihonjinron* popularizers.

A much easier work to comprehend is Toyama's (1976) collection of essays on the uniqueness of the language and the difficulty of translating it. Toyama starts with the Japanese expression *dearo*, an expression attached to the end of a sentence to soften the declarative nature of the sentence, rendering it a probable fact, and spends several pages showing how hard it is to translate this term into English. Even innocent particles, such as *ga, wa, no* (Oide 1965: 135–201) are sources of uniqueness of the language, let alone such cultural concepts as *amae* (Doi 1971), *ki* (Doi 1971: 108–116; Itasaka 1978: 129–137), and *iki* (Kuki 1930), which we have examined earlier.

**Social Structure**

Because the Japanese language requires predicate endings that show the relative status between the speaker and the listener, Japanese are said to be highly sensitive to relative social status in face-to-face interaction. The use of honorifics of varying degrees to indicate the specific relationship between the speaker and the listener is a widely known Japanese practice (Kindaichi 1957: 141-159; Yamashita 1979: 157–222).

Kindaichi also cites a variety of Japanese kinship and related terms to show their unique social meanings (1957: 149–159). That Japanese has two sets of distinct sibling terms depending on relative age – one set for older brother and sister (*ani* or *oniisan* and *ane* or *oneesan*) and another set for younger brother and sister (*otōto* and *imōto*) – is an expression of the recognized status difference between older and younger siblings. *Metoru*, denoting taking of a bride into a family, and *totsugu*, meaning marriage of a bride into a family, also indicate social structure, whereby patrilocal postmarital residence is the norm. Terms referring to the speaker, to the addressee, and to a third person referred to in the conversation need to be calibrated to the appropriate relationship among the three. Verb endings also vary depending on similar status considerations.

**Logicality**

The Japanese are so much concerned with avoiding conflict, according to Itasaka, that in Japanese communication, logic is sacrificed in favor of creating a harmonious mood (1978: 106). Much debate has raged over whether or not Japanese is a 'logical' language (Oide 1965; Toyama 1973). In the immediate postwar years of the late 1940s and the 1950s, Japanese *Nihonjinron* writers commonly argued that Japanese is not a logical language, holding up European languages such as English and French as examples of logical language par excellence. As will be argued in Chapter Seven, this position is a reflection of the inferiority the Japanese felt toward the West in the postwar years because of the country's defeat in the Pacific War. It is interesting that coinciding with Japan's economic recovery and success, arguments have been advanced that Japanese language has its own logic. Ōide's book on this point (1965), a forerunner of this point of view, went through eighteen printings in the first ten years after its publication. Ōide, philosopher and logician that he is, argues that Japanese expressions are not illogical, they simply do not make explicit some of the premises of their arguments, depending on the listener to infer them. Thus the arguments only appear illogical.

A similar view is expressed by Toyama, a professor of English literature, in his contrast between what he calls 'point logic' and 'line logic' (1973). By this Toyama means that in Japan intimate and close individuals need not verbalize all the details. All one need to do is to make points, skipping intermediate premises, and the listener understands by linking the points. This is 'point logic,' which supposedly characterizes the Japanese communication pattern. On the other hand, among those who are not so well acquainted, an unbroken line of reasoning has to be drawn from the beginning to the conclusion (1973: 13–14). This 'line logic' is, according to Toyama, the common pattern used by Europeans (1973: 17, 71, 151–155).

**Communication Pattern**

Much has been said about a certain uncanny ability of the Japanese to communicate with one another nonverbally, often expressed in Japanese as *ishin denshin* ('from mind to mind') or *haragei* ('belly art') (Itasaka 1978; Kunihiro 1988). Foreigners, lacking this ability, are thus by nature hindered in communicating with Japanese, according to this line of reasoning.

To bring home the point about this Japanese penchant for nonverbal communication, Itasaka (1978: 29) refers to one of the great literary figures of modern Japan, Kikuchi Kan, who often used '.........' in his novels to illustrate nonverbal communication among Japanese. Itasaka also maintains that a Japanese couple would not say 'I love you' to one another, since this is presumably understood, while in the West, husband and wife must continually reiterate this expression because, according to him, for them verbalization is the only way to communicate the idea of love. 'In a culture deficit in intuitive understanding,' according to him, 'the facile belief that "something like this should be understood without saying so" would not hold' (1978: 142). Itasaka (1978: 18–24) argues that Japanese culture not only deemphasizes verbal communication but also places positive value on nonverbal aspects of communication. In short, silence is golden. He brings out the Noh play as a case in point, saying that in Noh, emotions are expressed with the slightest of movements. Further, the Noh mask is not symmetrical right and left, the face being divided into ying and yang. The eye on the yang side is horizontal, but that on the ying side looks slightly downward. The cheeks and lips, too, show slight asymmetry. He cites a television commercial for an eyedrop medicine in which a Noh mask was shown from the ying side first; after medication, the yang side with a smile was shown. The slight asymmetry enables the actor to express different moods and emotions by exploiting the difference (1978: 21–22).

What enables this nonverbal communication, which foreigners are supposedly incapable of, is the body of unstated and implicit assumptions of which Oide speaks. A claim is made that the homogeneity of the culture in which the Japanese live enables them to communicate so well nonverbally, since the received culture they presumably all share is in fact the major premise of their logic. As long as the shared culture serves as the context in which verbal messages are to be understood, verbal messages need not be complete. So the argument goes.

## Cultural and Racial Origins

The curiosity of the general public about the origins of the Japanese people never ceases. Producers of Japan's identity discourse take advantage of the insatiable appetite of the public by providing endless reading materials. Archaeology is a particularly fascinating topic, for roots of the Japanese are manifested in a concrete way through excavated artifacts. Toward this effort, archaeology, both prehistoric and historic, makes major contributions. In addition, the biological anthropology and historical linguistics of the Japanese, as well as the ethnohistory or cultural history of the Japanese people, are brought in to play their respective roles.

We have already visited Egami Namio's hypothesis, claiming conquest of Japan during the proto-historic Tomb period by horseback-riding pastoralists from Inner Asia. As far as language origins are concerned, the standard understanding is that Japanese is part of the Altaic language group. Japanese linguists, however, have advanced the theory of 'language mixture,' whereby a Malayo-Polynesian (Austronesian) language and an Altaic language mixed, not only lexically but syntactically, to create a unique language called Japanese. This sort of syntactical language mixture is unheard of in Western linguistic theory, but it is advanced among Japanese scholars with all earnestness. Against the received idea of the Altaic affiliation of Japanese, linguist Ōno Susumu has proposed the theory of the Tamil origin of Japanese, which livened up the popular media because of its controversial nature (Ōno 1981).

As for cultural origins, Ueyama Shumpei, Sasaki Kōmei, Nakao Sasuke, and others have proposed the idea of 'a culture associated with a forest of shiny leaves' (*shōyō jurin bunka*). A floral belt consisting of such trees as camellia, oak, and other trees with evergreen, shiny leaves constitutes an arc in south China, the eastern edge of which reaches southern Japan. These cultural historians have found numerous common practices throughout this belt. For them, then, at least one important strain of Japanese culture derives from southern China (Ueyama, Sasaki, and Nakao 1976; Nakao and Sasaki 1992).

Regarding the 'racial' origins of the Japanese, again, many, many popular publications adorn shelves of bookstores. To take just one example, about twenty years ago physical anthropologist Hanihara Kazurō edited a popular book on where the Japanese came from (Hanihara ed. 1982). This book is based on a series of lectures delivered to the general public prominent scholars in biological anthropology, cultural history, archaeology, and linguistics. Among the authors, Hanihara, the major contributor to the volume, was then a professor at Tokyo University; he subsequently joined the International Research Center for Japanese Studies in Kyoto. Umehara Takeshi, who contributed a chapter on the thesis that the Ainu and Japanese languages are related, was then president of Kyoto Municipal University of Arts and later became director-general of the International Research Center. Philosopher Ueyama Shumpei, who discusses the geist of the Japanese state in this book, was director of the prestigious Research Institute of Humanistic Sciences of Kyoto University (see also Hanihara 1995, 1996, 1997).

The latest perhaps in the contribution of biological anthropology to Japan's cultural origins is Takeuchi Kumiko's argument (1999) that adult T-cell leukemia (ATL), common among the Ainu and presumably among the prehistoric Jōmon people but rare among neighboring Asiatic peoples, propagates through sexual intercourse and maternal milk-feeding. Takeuchi comes close to saying that the Japanese need for mutual dependency, a la Doi, is caused by ATL needing hosts for propagation: the more dependent they are on each other and the greater the chance of sexual intercourse, the better chance of ATL to propagate. This type of bio-teleological argument is always suspect. But Takeuchi writes well and marshals forth data from wide-ranging fields – from physiology, primatology, folklore, and ethnology – to try to persuade the reader.

Bruce Trigger (1989) classifies archaeologies of the world as 'colonial,' 'imperialistic,' and 'nationalistic.' In this scheme of things, Japanese archaeology is by and large nationalistic in the sense that much of the archaeological enterprise in Japan is directly tied in with clarifying and establishing the origins and the history of the Japanese people. This contrasts with much of the archaeology done in the United States, for example, where excavations are of Native American sites, and clarification of the origins and history of Native Americans is not directly related to the history of the vast majority of the country's population or of the investigators themselves.

Because archaeological activities in Japan are directly tied in with the ethnic origins and history of the contemporary Japanese, they are of absorbing interest for the public (Fawcett 1995, 1996). News of the discovery of new prehistoric sites and their historical significance adorn nationally circulated newspapers just about every week, often making headlines on the front page. When and whence did the Japanese migrate to the Japanese archipelago? What language did they speak then? What is the historic relationship between the Ainu and the Japanese? How was the Japanese culture derived from the Asiatic continent, how old is it, and is it related, say, to the Mongolian culture? Questions and curiosity continue endlessly. Archaeologists, linguists, biological anthropologists, and cultural historians all play major roles in satisfying the voracious appetite of the general public with scores of publications for laypeople every year.

In November 2000, archaeologist Fujimura Shin'ichi confessed to burying stone artifacts secretly, and making faked Paleolithic discoveries. In his confession, he said he felt strong pressure from the media to unearth major finds. Thus the hoax was a result of extraordinary public interest in the prehistory of Japan manifested in the intense media concern. Given such intensity of public interest in the prehistoric past, it is not beyond understanding if an archaeologist, hungry for public recognition, buries Paleolithic artifacts to be 'discovered' by himself, gaining the reputation as a 'god' of archaeology for his uncanny ability to identify the location of as yet unseen stone tools. When the hoax was revealed, the intense public interest warranted front page headlines in all major newspapers of national circulation.

Among all archaeological finds, one of the most important for *Nihonjinron* is the discovery of the oldest pottery in the world, dating back roughly 12,000 B.P. This find establishes Japan as having a unique place in the prehistory of the world. More recently, existence of even older pottery has been suggested by Japanese archaeologists, though this claim awaits substantiation.

At the northern extremity of the Honshu island is located the Sannai Daimaru site of the Jōmon period (ca. 12,000 B.P. to 2300 B.P.), which had been known from the Tokugawa period to produce prehistoric artifacts. But systematic excavations in the last ten years have begun to reveal the true magnitude of the site (Okada and Kōyama eds. 1996). About five hectares have been excavated so far, and this is believed to be only about one-seventh of the prehistoric settlement. Investigators uncovered six post holes as large as two meters in diameter, forming a rectangle. These posts were sunk two meters deep into the ground, supporting an enormous structure. This discovery and numerous artifacts imply that occupants of this site led a sedentary life, rather than a nomadic existence as previously assumed for the Jōmon period foragers. It is estimated that the site represents fifteen hundred years of continuous occupation from the Early to Middle Jōmon period. This site is now made into a park for permanent exhibition of the way of life of the Jōmon people in order to satisfy the intense interest of the contemporary Japanese in their prehistoric past, which helps define their historical identity.

It is curious that Japanese archaeologists, in relating their interpretations of Japan's prehistory to the general public, do not very much bring out Korean connections. It is well known that in the Yayoi and Tomb periods (2300 B.P. to 1400 B.P.), southern Japan and southern Korea shared large quantities of cultural elements. Some scholars go so far as to say that they constituted a single culture area. Huge royal tombs, jewelry, and other ornaments that characterize the Yayoi and Tomb cultures are also widely found in southern Korea. Yet most Japanese are under the impression that Japan has been a distinct culture from early prehistoric times. In the meantime, Korean prehistorians and cultural historians are busy discovering common cultural factors and have even advanced the theory that Japan is a mere appendage to Korea, which supplied virtually all Japan has. While all this serves Korean nationalism well, such a view does not sit well with *Nihonjinron* writers, and no doubt would not be well received by the Japanese in the current political climate of Japanese-Korean relations.

In 1989, the Yoshinogari site in Saga prefecture, Kyūshū, belonging to the late Yayoi period and covering an area two kilometers by five kilometers, was uncovered. This became major media news because of the richness of the remains, the unprecedented scale of the site, and its implications for interpreting the prehistory of Japan. *Asahi Graph*, a popular pictorial magazine, published a special issue with numerous photographs of the site and artifacts, exploring the meaning of this discovery. The magazine invited such notables as archaeologist Mori Kōichi, science fiction writer Matsumoto Seichō, and historian of ancient Japan Okuno Masao to speculate on such tantalizing issues as the possibility that the site might represent the phantom state of Yamatai, mentioned in a Chinese document but never identified in Japan; on the political hegemony the site might have extended throughout northern Kyūshū, and on the extent of military prowess the site might have demonstrated.

Another impressive site, once again from the Jōmon period, is Daimaru-Sannai in Aomori Prefecture. This site, too, covers an immense area, where hundreds of people are said to have lived in a sedentary community in continuous occupation at least for several generations. Findings at this site controverted the received view that the Jōmon hunters were a nomadic people living in small groups and constantly moving from place to place in search of food. These and other major sites are made into archaeological parks, where Japanese visit half as curious tourists and half as pilgrims paying homage.

## Feminist *Nihonjinron*

Examining much of the *Nihonjinron* literature, what I find singularly lacking is *Nihonjinron* from the feminist perspective. I have encountered virtually none among the hundreds of books I have examined, whether by male or female authors or by Japanese or foreigners, which tried to give women's points of view on the Japanese identity. How, for example, does the much-touted group orientation of the Japanese appear from women's position? Women are absent from much of the hierarchy of the corporate structure that is taken as the prime manifestation of the Japanese groupism. Most women are at the bottom rung in corporate structure or they are at home. Is the esthetics of the Japanese culture, such as the concept of *iki* (Kuki 1930), the same for women as for men?

It is interesting that even among the several critiques, reviews, and histories of Nihonjinron, this total absence of women's perspective has never been made an issue, possibly because authors of such critiques, reviews, and histories are all men. It is even more interesting that Japanese – or foreign – feminists have not proposed a feminine or feminist version of *Nihonjinron*.

This is by no means to say that feminist literature is absent in Japan. On the contrary, at least since around 1970, feminist scholarship has burgeoned, giving rise to feminism as a recognized genre in the publishing industry. Well-known feminist scholars have been quite active in critiquing gender issues in Japan –

historically, socially, and culturally. Yet they seem to shy away from participating in the *Nihonjinron* discourse. Thus the genre remains dominated by men and arguments represent male, though not necessarily patriarchal, perspectives.

In this chapter I have merely skimmed the surface of the content of *Nihonjinron* without being able to do justice to all the fascinating contributions, not even all of the major ones, due to limitations of space. But enough has been presented for the reader to glimpse what the Japanese refer to when they discuss the uniqueness of their character, their culture, and their society. Some of the propositions in this identity discourse seem somewhat far-fetched even to a casual reader, while others can stand up to scientific scrutiny. It is not the task here to pass judgment on these propositions. In the next chapter we will look into the nature of the literature in which Japanese present their identity discourse and discuss the producers of this literature.

# 3 The Literature

Granted that *Nihonjinron* has to do with the search for the essence of being Japanese, or the uniqueness of Japanese culture, in what sources do the Japanese find *Nihonjinron*? In this chapter we shall not concern ourselves with content of *Nihonjinron*, which has been elaborated in the previous chapter. Instead, here we are interested in examining the media in which it appears, its producers, and its consumers.

## Sources

*Nihonjinron* as a form of cultural discourse is expressed not only in books but in a variety of other forms as well. Books, magazines, public lectures, roundtable discussions, television and radio programs, and college courses are some of the formal contexts in which *Nihonjinron* is presented in Japan. Above all, when they travel abroad and when they entertain foreigners – situations where Japaneseness is called into question in stark contrast, the Japanese are likely to talk and think about aspects of *Nihonjinron*.

According to the survey Manabe Kazufumi and I conducted in Nishinomiya in 1987, more respondents expressed interest in *Nihonjinron* in newspapers and on television than on radio or in magazines or books (Befu and Manabe 1989, 1991, 1998).[10] Many people who do not bother to read about *Nihonjinron* in books or magazines still read about it in newspapers and watch programs about *Nihonjinron* on television because of the accessibility of these sources: newspapers are daily delivered to one's home, and the television in the sitting room delivers *Nihonjinron* by a simple push of a button.

Publications such as *Chūō Kōron*, *Bungei Shunjū*, *Sekai*, *Shokun*, *Seiron*, and other popular magazines for the general public offer *Nihonjinron* articles as staples. The 1970–74 cumulative index to Japanese periodicals published by the National Diet Library contain two closely related sections relevant here. One is *Nihonjin/*

*Nihonjinron*, the other, *Nihonron/Nihonkan*, the latter meaning 'views on Japan.' This is about the only more or less comprehensive compilation of magazine articles on the subject. (These headings were done away with after 1974.) If we combine the two categories, the total number of titles listed in this five-year period is 245. Even granting ebbs and flows in the popularity of *Nihonjinron* – and the 1970s was a period of heightened interest in the subject – many times this number of articles must have been published in the whole of the postwar period. If we add articles in newspapers to these magazine articles, we are likely to have thousands of publications.

For the analysis of *Nihonjinron* discourse in this book, I have chosen to rely, by and large, on monographs, and secondarily on magazine and newspaper articles. Reasons are simple and pragmatic. First, books are much more convenient to use and easier to locate than ephemeral newspaper and magazine articles. Also, given their length, books can present ideas more systematically and comprehensively. Radio and television programs are fleeting and transcripts difficult to secure. Given the staggering number of books on the topic – well over a thousand since 1945 – monographs alone can supply an adequate sampling of the literature. Finally, discussion on *Nihonjinron* appearing in newspaper and magazine articles and on radio and television programs is quite often transformed into a book by the same people who have presented it in other formats, often refining and expanding their ideas. For example, Katō Shūichi's work on Nihonjinron (1976) is a collection of articles that originally appeared in magazines or as parts of other books. A series of public lectures sponsored by Nihon Nōritsu Kyōkai was given in 1982 by a number of noted intellectuals on *Nihonjinron*. The series was published within a year in book form (T. Suzuki, Nitoda, and Kawakami 1983).

## Titles

Publishers tell us that the title is half the sales strategy in marketing a book. If the reader is thirsty for *Nihonjinron* books, there is no better strategy than to include '*Nihonjinron*' and related terms such as '*Nihon Bunkaron*' and '*Nihonron*' in the title, and such books are legion. One such book, titled *Nihon Bunkaron*, was authored by an eminent anthropologist of the past generation, Ishida Eiichirō (1969),[11] formerly on the Tokyo University faculty; and another with the identical title by another eminent scholar, Umehara Takeshi (1976). *Nihonjinron*, a book with another popular title edited by philosopher Ikumatsu Keizō (1977), contains papers by Miyake Setsurei and Haga Yaichi, two prominent *Nihonjinron* writers in the second half of the Meiji era – about the turn of the century. This is a vintage *Nihonjinron* work still in print.

Similarly, titles containing terms like *Nihon* (Japan) or *Nihonjin* (Japanese), are appealing to readers. There are five books with the identical, intriguing title of *Nihonjin to wa Nanika* (What Is, or Who Are the Japanese People?), one edited by the well-known literary critic Katō Shūichi (1976) referred to earlier, another edited by historian Egami Namio (Egami et al. ed. 1985), and a third by a former dean of personality psychology, Miyagi Otoya (1972), a fourth by Nakanishi Susumu (1997), and a fifth by Yamamoto Shichihei (1992). Books with similarly eye-catching titles abound. In translation, these titles become 'Puzzles of the Japanese' by well-known philosopher Tsurumi Shunsuke (1996), 'Japan's Political Climate,' by Shinohara Hajime (1968), 'That Which Is Japan-Like' by philosopher Shimizu Ikutarō (1968), 'Rediscovery of the Japanese' by Higuchi Kiyoyuki (1974a), one of the most prolific *Nihonjinron* writers, 'Japan and the Japanese' by historian Kaizuka Shigeki (1974), 'On Behalf of *Nihonjinron*' by Aizawa Hisashi (1976), and 'Japanese Culture and *Nihonjinron*' by philosopher Fukasaku Mitsusada (1971). The list goes on.

Nieda Rokusaburō (1975) deals with what he considers to be characteristic Japanese traits in belles lettres in a book titled *Nihonjin Jishin* (The Japanese Themselves). Kitagawa Tadaichi (1983), professor of human sciences at Tokiwa University at the time of writing, ponders over the historical roots of the formation of the Japanese national character. Watanabe Shōichi (1973), sometime professor at Sophia University in Tokyo, concerns himself with quintessential 'Japanliness' in his portrayal of the Japanese through the analysis of the Japanese history.

As we saw in Chapter Two, in the cultural anatomy of Japan, *kokoro* (heart) occupies a prominent place. Its venerable history in *Nihonjinron* goes back to the late Tokugawa period, when National Learning (*kokugaku*) scholars referred to *kokoro* as the anatomical site of the geist of Japanese culture. It is through the probing of this heart of Japan that many writers propound their *Nihonjinron*. No wonder then that so many books bear the term *kokoro* in their titles (Furukawa 1978; Goi 1973; Karaki 1965; Maruyama 1991; Nakazawa 1995; Okazaki 1981; Tsurumi ed. 1997; Umesao et al. 1974; Wakamori 1981; Yasuda and Nakagawa 1969; Yoshida 1996).

In addition to these books, which deal with *Nihonjinron* globally, others deal with certain subgenres within *Nihonjinron* such as language, race, culture, and cultural origins. Many of these have already been introduced in Chapter Two.

The popularity of *Nihonjinron* is seen also in the publication of magazines devoted to *Nihonjinron* discourse. Characteristically, these magazines have such titles as *Nihon to Nihonjin* (Japan and the Japanese), *Nihon oyobi Nihonjin* (Japan and the Japanese), *Nihonjin*, *Nihongaku: The Quarterly of Japanology*, and *Nihon Bunka* (Japanese Culture).

There are, in fact, two series bearing the title *Nihon Bunka*, one begun in 1937 but discontinued during the war years and the other begun in 1977. The first one, being produced at the height of Japan's militaristic nationalism, is highly nationalistic and patriotic in content. The second, published by the Research Institute of Japanese Culture, began its issues in the era of Japan's 'internationalization.' As a magazine attempting to meet the needs of an 'internationalizing Japan,' it 'examines Japanese culture from all angles of international perspectives, while at the same time reaffirming the identity of the Japanese,' according to editorial comments in the inaugural issue. As such, it includes comments and articles by foreigners, especially those who are well known, and deals with topics of international importance for Japanese as well as those relating to their cultural identity. Topics range widely – for example, international marriage, Japanese children who have spent many years abroad, multinational firms, foreign students in Japan, samurai of the warring period of the sixteenth century, origins of the Japanese language, and education in Japan – but all are topics of vital importance for *Nihonjinron*.

## Popularity

*Nihonjinron* is popular in part because every Japanese has some view or idea about Japan and the Japanese. Most Japanese are capable of, as it were, taking the sentence completion test: 'The

Japanese are – ' or 'Important features of Japanese culture are – .' Thus it is a topic nearly everyone has some opinion about, and because most Japanese have an interest in the topic, a very strong one at times, publications on the topic abound and are widely sold. The relatively low intellectual level of these publications compared with the rigor of academic writing standards is obviously to accommodate the lowest common denominator of the *Nihonjinron* readership. This is not to say that there are not highly stimulating, profound writings on the subject, of course, but they constitute the tip of a pyramid – the lower the quality, the more numerous the publications.

Though the 1987 Nishinomiya survey mentioned earlier is somewhat old, in the absence of more recent data, we rely on it to explore the extent of popularity of *Nihonjinron*. Eighty-two percent of those who responded said that they were indeed interested in the subject and read about it in the newspaper, and smaller percentages found other media, such as television, magazine, radio, and books, useful in this regard. Only 51 percent read books to satisfy their curiosity.

*Nihonjinron* arguments in newspapers are not much different from those in monographs. One thing is sure to be different: newspaper articles have to be much shorter than monographs – no more than a few column inches – equivalent to one or two monograph pages. Because of this, newspaper articles tend to deal with *Nihonjinron* much more superficially than monographs on the subject, depicting characteristics of Japanese culture in easily understandable stereotypes and clichés much more than monographs do.

Since the number of copies of a book sold is generally a trade secret and not readily available, the next best gauge is the number of printings a book goes through. I surveyed publishers and gathered data on this matter in 1989. Of the 151 titles for which usable data were supplied by publishers, 58 were hardcover and 93, paperback. Ninety-one of the 151 titles had been reprinted fewer than ten times, but the remaining 60 titles, or well over one-third, have been reprinted ten times or more – a rather impressive record. Two hardcovers and three paperbacks had been reprinted more than fifty times. Though we are not primarily concerned with *Nihonjinron* by foreigners – our focus is on the self-identity of the Japanese – I cannot refrain from pointing out that the number-one best-seller, combining soft and hard covers, is the 1948 Japanese translation of Ruth Benedict's *The Chrysanthemum and the Sword* (1946). Translations have seen ten different editions, and altogether the ten editions produced a minimum of 146 printings as of 1989.[12] According to an article reviewing postwar *Nihonjinron* literature by foreigners in the Japanese edition of *Newsweek* (January 31, 1996), 2.3 million copies of this classic have been sold, surpassing its closest rival, the Japanese translation (Vogel 1979b) of Ezra Vogel's *Japan as Number One* (1979a), by a factor of almost four. Of course, *The Chrysanthemum and the Sword* has been in print the longest in the postwar period. Still and all, the record is impressive. Few Japanese *Nihonjinron* writers can afford not to read or at least pay homage to this classic. It is a sine qua non accouterment of Japanese intelligentsia. Benedict's views on Japanese culture are, in one way or another, reflected in most *Nihonjinron* writings by Japanese, whether they endorse or refute her claims. One is tempted to claim that the postwar anthropology of Japan is in large part made up of footnotes to Benedict's classic.

Another much-touted *Nihonjinron* work is the aforementioned *Nihonjin to Yudayajin* (The Japanese and the Jews) by Isaiah BenDasan (1970). In 1984, Yamamoto Shichihei, the creator of BenDasan and his work, revealed in a interview in weekly magazine *Asahi Jānaru* (June 22, pp. 6–7) that about 1.75 million copies of this book, hard and soft covers combined, had been sold. As of 1989, the hardcover alone had been reprinted fifty times. Doi Takeo's '*Amae*' *no Kōzō* (Anatomy of Dependence) (1971), the third most popular on our list, had seen 147 printings by 1989. Three others that have gone through more than fifty printings are the Japanese versions of Nakane's *Japanese Society* (1970), Watsuji's *A Climate: A Philosophical Study* (1961), and Suzuki Daisetz's *Zen and the Japanese Culture* (1959), respectively Nakane (1967), Watsuji (1935), and D. Suzuki (1940). These books are true long-sellers, still found in bookstores. *Nihonjinron* books are sold widely at bookstores catering to the general public. Larger bookstores have a special section dedicated to books on *Nihonjinron*, where hundreds of titles are displayed.

While we have surmised the popularity of *Nihonjinron* books, up to now we have had no empirical studies to demonstrate to what extent *Nihonjinron*, spun out mostly by armchair scholars and other intellectuals, is in fact being read by ordinary people. In a way, we have had an outpouring of *Nihonjinron* discussion in all media without any knowledge about effects on common people. Studies of *Nihonjinron* so far, in other words, have been studies of *Nihonjinron* as a consumer product, so to speak, but not of consumer reaction.

In our Nishinomiya survey, Manabe and I listed twenty-one popular books in *Nihonjinron* and asked respondents to tell us which authors they had heard of, which titles they had heard of, and which books they had read. The writers included Aida Yūji, Isaiah BenDasan, Ruth Benedict, Doi Takeo, Herman Kahn, Donald Keene, Kindaichi Haruhiko, Nakane Chie, and Edwin Reischauer. Except for Kindaichi Haruhiko, whose name was known to more than half of the respondents, none of these writers was known to more than 41 percent of the respondents. Still, to be known by 40 percent of the sample, if extrapolated to the whole of the adult Japanese population, would mean that millions of Japanese adults are familiar with an author, a creditable number.

Only five authors besides Kindaichi were known by more than a quarter of respondents.[13] None of the twenty-one books had been read by more than a quarter of the respondents. Only three books had been read by more than 10 percent.[14] These figures may seem disappointingly low for those who think *Nihonjinron* is an all-consuming topic among the Japanese. But again, extrapolating to the population, even 10 percent would mean millions of Japanese have read some of these books – a rather staggering popularity. As we try to assess the significance of *Nihonjinron* among ordinary Japanese, it is important to appreciate the large numbers *Nihonjinron* books sold and the multitudes of people, who read them, but at the same time not to exaggerate its popularity.

## Contributors to the Literature

As is evident from the *Nihonjinron* authors and their books already cited, contributors to this enterprise run the gamut of the Japanese intelligentsia. The following is a representative example.

In 1979 a symposium was held to explore the basic nature of Japanese culture, origins of the Japanese, and other topics in *Nihonjinron*. Its proceedings were published the following year (Egami et al. 1980). The glittering roster of participants of this symposium, including some already introduced to us, reads like Japan's intellectual Who's Who:

- Egami Namio, professor emeritus of Tokyo University, who took the public by surprise with his now well-known 'equestrian theory' of the origin of the Japanese state (Egami 1967)
- Itō Shuntarō, formerly of Tokyo University and then of the International Center for Japanese Studies, and former president of the International Society for Civilization Studies
- Kawai Hayao, professor emeritus of Kyoto University and now director-general of the International Center for Japanese Studies, and author of a number of books on Japanese personality, identity, and psychological problems (Kawai 1976, 1984)
- Miyagi Otoya, formerly of the Tokyo Institute of Technology, the doyen of Japanese personality psychology and author of numerous popular books on the Japanese, especially in comparison with Americans (Miyagi 1972, 1976)
- Mori Kōichi of Doshisha University, an archaeologist who has done much to popularize Japanese archaeology
- Nakane Chie, formerly of Tokyo University and already familiar to us
- Ōno Susumu of Gakushūin University (where members of the imperial family attend), a linguist who has propounded popular theories of origins of the Japanese language (Ōno 1957, 1974)
- Ueda Masaaki of Kyoto University, well-known historian on the origin of the Japanese state and author of numerous books on Japanese myths
- Ueyama Shumpei of Kyoto University, a philosopher who has broadly written on many aspects of Japanese history and prehistory (Ueyama 1971, 1980)
- Umehara Takeshi, formerly of Kyoto City University of Arts and former director-general of the International Center for Japanese Studies, who has expressed many controversial views on the origins of the Japanese culture and people (Umehara 1976, 1984)

Many *Nihonjinron* authors, like those listed here, are figures well known to the general public – famous scholars teaching at prestigious universities, directors or staff of prestigious research institutions, authors of numerous popular books, and social or literary critics. Some are presidents and executives of well-known companies. For example, Idemitsu Sazō, founder, president, and chairman of Idemitsu Kōsan – the only wholly Japanese-owned oil company – wrote a book urging the Japanese to return spiritually to their Japanese 'home' (Idemitsu 1971). It is for this reason that in writing on *Nihonjinron*, Yoshino Kōsaku (1992) interviewed a number of businessmen to extract their views on *Nihonjinron*.

Other *Nihonjinron* writers are freelance intellectuals known as *hyōronka* (critics). *Hyōronka* make their living by writing popular books and magazine and newspaper articles, giving lectures, and appearing on television and radio programs. Many of them have little formal training in the area of claimed expertise but nonetheless have made their fame by writing for the public in certain specialized topics, be it food, fashion, health, air traffic, or equipment for the handicapped.

As if to give added credence to the 'science' of *Nihonjinron*, hard scientists and Nobel Prize winners have wittingly or unwittingly joined the ranks of *Nihonjinron* contributors. Their views are assumed to have a quantum-level higher degree of truth than views of soft scientists like anthropologists, sociologists, and psychologists and even softer humanists like historians and literary critics, putting them well beyond challenge by laypeople. Robert J. Smith (1983: 111) quotes Nobel laureate in physics Yukawa Hideki as uttering a piece in *Nihonjinron* that the Japanese avoid any form of rational compromise based on a selection from among alternative possibilities. Ezaki Renoa, also a Nobel Prize winner in physics, was a regular contributor to the *Yomiuri Shinbun* when he resided in the United States before taking up the presidency of Tsukuba University. In these essays he was fond of making global, essentialized statements about the Japanese, comparing them with Americans. We have already encountered the hemispheric theory of Japanese linguistic competence by physician Tsunoda (1978) in the preceding chapter.

We should not denigrate the works of *hyōronka* and college professors. They perform an important function in Japanese society. They translate specialized scholarly findings in whatever fields – from medicine and aeronautics to literary criticism and archaeology – for the general public and make such findings comprehensible to those who do not have the specialized training to understand more erudite and technical writings. This role of the intellectual educating and enlightening the less educated has a legitimate place in Japanese society. Although the simplification of complex ideas in this process sometimes results in bastardization and caricaturization, nonetheless, with a single, compact paperback, these writers can and do inform and influence those who would do not have the time or inclination to study the subject matter in depth on their own. Readers, television viewers, and lecture audiences become exposed to various views of Japanese culture, thanks to *Nihonjinron* popularizers. To the extent that their interpretations are accepted by the public, they are influential figures.

Too, scholars' writings in such media often turn out to be solid scholarship, rather than shoddy writing, and are later recognized for their contributions and are cited in scholarly publications. Scholars very often experiment with their scholarly ideas first in popular sources – sometimes in paperback books and sometimes in magazines such as *Chūō Kōron* or *Sekai*. The basic ideas in Nakane's best-selling book on 'the vertical society' (1967) were first published in *Chūō Kōron* (Nakane 1964). Similarly, Aoki's serialized articles in *Chūō Kōron* (1989a, 1989b) became the basis of his award-winning book on the postwar history of *Nihonjinron* (1990).

One should not underestimate the pecuniary motive and the desire for recognition by the general public among scholars and other *Nihonjinron* writers. For more popular writers, royalties and honoraria for public speeches amount to a sizeable portion of their income. The role of scholars in Japanese society is somewhat different from that in North America, where they generally do not seek public recognition. The vast majority of North American scholars shy away from appearing on television or radio, and from writing regular newspaper columns or articles for popular magazines that would lead to their being labeled as popularizers. At the same time, in North America, the media do not seek out scholars, except when an incident occurs, such as an airplane crash or a major earthquake.

Japanese intellectuals – 'the scholars (*gakusha*),' 'the teachers (*sensei*),' 'the men and women of culture (*bunkajin*),' and 'the people of knowledge (*chishikijin*),' as they are reverently called – are important opinion leaders and are listened to carefully. As

Herbert Passin once said, when they are in the 'salon,' their presence graces the occasion and validates the cause. Scholars are constantly in demand in the media. Monthlies like *Chūō Kōron* and *Sekai* regularly feature several articles by scholars. Newspapers of national circulation, such as *Asahi* and *Mainichi*, are adorned with articles written by university professors almost every day. What they write in newspapers is very often quite innocuous or even trivial – something anyone of average intelligence can write. What 'just anyone' cannot supply is the value added to the article because of the prestige of the name of the well-known scholar circulated as a household name. Readers read to partake in the private life of a famous person revealed in tidbits in the article. The paper earns status by printing the name of a prestigious intellectual and in turn the intellectual earns a handsome honorarium, scaled to his or her prestige. College professors who write *Nihonjinron* for popular consumption are taking part in this more general outreach function and prestige structure of the scholarly community.

## Foreigners' Participation

A word needs to be said about foreigners' participation in *Nihonjinron*. This book is concerned with *Nihonjinron* as an expression of Japanese self-identity. Despite the vast literature on *Nihonjinron* by foreigners, therefore, we are not interested in foreigners' *Nihonjinron* works unless they shed light on the question of Japanese self-identity. If foreigners' writings in the *Nihonjinron* genre are in foreign languages, their effects on the Japanese in general is minimal because although Japanese do study foreign languages, notably English, in the course of their formal education, most of them do not acquire enough proficiency to read with ease anything beyond a few printed pages. Consequently, most books on Japan whose subject matter is *Nihonjinron* but whose language is not Japanese are unread by most Japanese or even unknown to them. Thus, the effects of foreign writers on the general public is indirect at best, as when a Japanese *Nihonjinron* writer, reading them in the original foreign language, introduces the foreign authors' ideas or incorporates them into writings in Japanese.

Most Japanese are keenly interested in the Otherness of themselves, or perhaps even obsessed by how foreigners, especially

Westerners, see them. This obsession with foreigners' views of Japan is seen in the almost regularly produced books by Japanese on how Japan is viewed in foreign lands as well as in the large number of translations of books on Japan originally written in foreign languages for the postwar period (for example, Ayabe ed. 1992; Benedict 1946; Konaka 1997; Besshi 1999; Satō 1997; Murakami 1997). It is precisely because of the Japanese eagerness to learn what foreigners have to say about the Japanese that so many books in the genre of *Nihonjinron* by foreigners are translated into Japanese.

Although most of these books have only moderate sales and never reach the best-seller list in the foreign countries where they are originally published, their Japanese versions usually enjoy brisk sales and even reach the best-seller list there, as with the Japanese translations of Benedict's *The Chrysanthemum and the Sword* (1946), Reischauer's *The Japanese* (1978) and Vogel's *Japan as Number One* (1979a), respectively Benedict (1948), Reischauer (1979), and Vogel (1979b).

The intense Japanese interest in foreigners' views on Japan has deep roots. Because of Japan's peripheral position throughout most of its history, it has always been at the receiving end of more advanced cultures: Japan has always looked to more advanced civilizations for ideas and technology. In early historic times, the Asiatic continent, notably Korea and China, have been the sources of advanced civilization. More recently, of course, the West has replaced East Asia as the source of the ideas and technology. Thus the desire to read foreign and especially Western accounts of Japan is part of a more general inferiority-complex-based interest in things foreign. This issue is important for understanding the history of *Nihonjinron* and will be taken up in Chapter Seven.

In the aforementioned bibliography of *Nihonjinron* compiled by Nomura Research Institute in 1978, some 100 of the 698 titles are translations of books by foreigners. Thus, if we are to trust this compilation at all, one out of seven *Nihonjinron* books published in the thirty-three-year period since the end of World War II was contributed by a foreigner. This enormous interest in foreigners' views of Japan is also expressed in a bibliographic series on *Nihonjinron* titled *Sekai no Nihonjinkan* (Views on the Japanese in the World), compiled by Chikushi Tetsuya (1982). Dedicated solely to listing Japanese translations of foreign-language books on the topic, the 1982 edition boasts 110 titles with two-to-three page annotations and 70 additional titles with shorter annotations, this being the fourth edition, and was annually updated until 1986. Although authors on this list make up quite an international assortment – including those from Australia, Belgium, China, France, Hungary, Israel, Italy, Korea, Spain, the United Kingdom, the United States, and the former Soviet Union – an overwhelming number of them are of Western European nationality, and a great majority of them are American, for reasons that should be obvious by now. Another similar book, by Murakami Katsutoshi (1997), takes up twenty-two postwar *Nihonjinron* books by foreign authors, only one of whom is non-Western.

One may compare this Japanese attitude with that of Americans, who are by and large oblivious of foreigners' assessment of American culture and society. This lack of interest by Americans in outsiders' views of themselves is evident in the almost total absence of books on America translated from foreign languages. De Tocqueville's *Democracy in America* (1954 [1835, 1840]) is a notable exception, however, that serves only to emphasize the point.

In considering foreigners' contributions to *Nihonjinron*, one must not ignore the interaction between Japanese and foreign authors of *Nihonjinron*. For example, Reischauer in his *Japanese Today* (1988) recommends among others Doi Takeo's *Anatomy of Dependence* and Nakane Chie's *Japanese Society*, the two books that have done most to popularize certain ideas about the Japanese or Japanese society. Ardath Burke, in his *Japan: A Profile of a Post-Industrial Power* (1980), cites Nakane's work in the back of the book as one of the books 'that have proved useful' to him. Frank Gibney in *Japan: The Fragile Superpower* (1979: 77, 108) and Zbigniew Brzezinski in *The Fragile Blossom* (1972: 33) both endorse Nakane's work. Robert Christopher, in *The Japanese Mind*, endorses Doi Takeo as 'perhaps the best known of contemporary Japanese psychiatrists' (1983: 73) and 'Japan's leading psychiatrist' (1983: 270). These references by foreigners give the Japanese authors a 'circular' eminence: they induce foreign readers to believe these Japanese writers' assertions about Japan and this 'international' reputation gives the named writers added eminence in Japan. Once these books are translated into

Japanese and added to *Nihonjinron* shelves in bookstores, these foreign authors' views become readily available to Japanese writers as well as to Japanese *Nihonjinron* readers.

Furthermore, many of the Japanese *Nihonjinron* writers are proficient enough in foreign languages to be able to read *Nihonjinron* literature in the original foreign languages. Conversely, many foreign writers in this genre are conversant enough with Japanese to discuss *Nihonjinron* issues with Japanese *Nihonjinron* writers and read *Nihonjinron* literature in Japanese. Moreover, a good deal of *Nihonjinron* literature authored by Japanese has been translated into or written in foreign languages, notably English. Works by Isaiah BenDasan (1972), Doi Takeo (1973), Hasegawa Nyozekan (1966), Ishida Eiichirō (1974), Nakamura Hajime (1965), Nakane Chie (1970), and Suzuki Daisetz (1938, 1959) are some of the more prominent examples. Some, such as Suzuki's *Zen and Japanese Culture* and Uchimura Kanzo's *Japannische Charaktersopfs: Rechtmassige Verdeutschung* (1908a) were originally written in foreign languages for foreign consumption and then translated into Japanese. Thus communication between Japanese and foreign writers of *Nihonjinron* is enhanced by mutual translation, direct communication, and reading each other's works in their original languages.

It is important to note once again, however, that although Japanese and foreigners may appear to be writing the same *Nihonjinron*, outsiders differ from insiders in their basic disposition. Outsiders see Japan as Other, often an exoticized Other. They either try to be objective in their observations or they criticize what is foreign to their standards of value. The vantage point is always that of the outsider. Japanese writers, on the other hand, are personally, emotionally, and subjectively involved in the subject matter. It is their own personal identity as derived from their culture that is at stake. They are talking about themselves when they write about *Nihonjinron*, not about some Other. The Japanese therefore take a deeply personal stance. Even though intellectuals who write *Nihonjinron* would like to distance themselves from the subject they write about and treat the subject matter of *Nihonjinron* as if it were someone else's identity, there is no escaping that the identity they propound or analyze in their writing is their own.

Nonetheless, the interaction between Japanese and foreign contributors to this genre makes it difficult to assume that *Nihonjinron* written by the Japanese expresses purely autochthonous views untrammeled by foreign 'contamination,' even though the ideas expressed generally emphasize Japan's traditional culture, which is said to be unique. One indeed finds common elements in both foreigners' and Japanese writers' *Nihonjinron*. For example, one of the salient features of *Nihonjinron* emphasized by many Japanese writers is Japanese groupism, which is also a point dwelled upon by many foreigners.

I submit, however, that there are different motives for emphasizing the same feature, say, Japanese groupism. Foreigners do so because it contrasts with Western individualism (Befu 1980). Foreigners, seeing Japan in their Orientalizing gaze, are quick to note the moral superiority of individualism over groupism, where to foreigners groupism implies blind obedience to group norms through smothering of individual rights and personal interests. This groupist characterization of Japan, then, is an essential part and parcel of the Western Orientalist image of Japan.

Japanese *Nihonjinron* writers make the same comparison, but for different motives: group orientation is an essential part of the consensual, harmonious model of Japanese society, which image the Japanese would like foreigners to believe because it puts the best foot of Japanese culture forward. It masks Japan's seamy side. It hides dirt under the rug and presents a facade of a well-ordered society.

## *Nihonjinron* as a Mass Culture Phenomenon

We go wrong if we think of *Nihonjinron* literature in the same vein as, say, scholarly works of the sociology of the family, the theory of the state, or literary criticism. We will find much of the literature in this field unable to sustain canons of scholarship practiced by most scholars. It is for this reason that so many foreign scholars are highly critical of the *Nihonjinron* literature, for example, Dale (1986), Miller (1982), and Mouer and Sugimoto (1986). Miller's criticisms are so sarcastic and ad hominem that he declines to name his Japanese collaborators in the acknowledgment section of the book for fear of putting them in jeopardy.

At the scholarly end of this continuum, one finds such works as Aruga Kizaemon's *Nihonjinron* essay (1976), Nakamura Hajime's treatise on the thought processes of the Japanese (1948–49), or the ambitious thesis by Murakami, Kumon, and Satō (1979) on the nature of Japanese civilization. These highly acclaimed studies can stand up to any test of scholarship. But these are technical works, published in small print runs, and are generally expensive and not readily accessible to the general public. Such works can be found only in a small number of academic bookstores and are read by only a small number of scholars and students.

Popular versions of *bunkaron* are distinguishable from scholarly works by several criteria (Befu 1997). First, they generally lack 'scholarly apparatus' – extensive citations, footnotes, bibliography, and so on. Such appendages make a book harder to write, more expensive to produce, and more cumbersome to read.

A second difference is that popular *Nihonjinron* writings are based on intuition and impressionistic observation, rather than on time-consuming analysis of large amounts of data, substantiation of hypotheses, or extensive reading of previous scholarly contributions in the field – all standard procedures in scholarly writing.

A third difference is that ideas in most *Nihonjinron* writings are simple and easy to comprehend. Stereotyping abounds in this genre. Discourses in this field are more like cocktail party conversations than seminar discussions, which is precisely why they appeal to the general public. Most popular *Nihonjinron* books are short – one hundred to two hundred pages. Even if the books are longer, contents tend to be a series of disparate observations and comments in segments, each of which can stand alone. One can read any short segment and understand the contents. A final difference is that most books in this genre are inexpensive. Most are paperbacks that sell for four hundred to one thousand yen – about the cost of a businessman's lunch or less – priced to make them affordable to anyone.

## Consumer Goods

If *Nihonjinron* literature constitutes a continuum from an erudite, scholarly end to a popular extreme, then how should we treat the *Nihonjinron* literature on the popular side of the continuum? I suggest that we regard it as consumer goods in a mass market, like swim suits, shirts, and neckties. These needs are, as we shall see, defined in terms of the desire of the Japanese to define their identity in an internationalizing and globalizing Japan in the context of Japanese economic expansion in the world.

What happens when we treat *Nihonjinron* like consumer goods? The raison d'ĕtre of consumer goods is sales: consumer goods must be sold for profit. However, perhaps because neither publishers nor writers conduct market surveys to determine the needs of consumers, many Nihonjinron books are short-lived, going out of stock without additional printings. But out of so many hundred titles, some are bound to be popular and sell well. When demand is great and supply meager, any product sells, and the large volume of sales in this genre may be due simply to the overwhelming demand of the consumers, whose voracious appetites must be satisfied with whatever is available, good or bad, tasteful or tasteless.

Moreover, a reason why there is little market research and explicit marketing strategy may be that in this genre, prescriptions for writing are relatively simple and clear. As we have seen, one of the most common and the easiest is to engage in arm-chair comparison of Japan with the West.

As we have seen, *Nihonjinron* books, like other mass-produced goods, are sold at a low cost so that just about anyone wishing them can have them. The basic principle is the economy of scale. Scholarly books, on the other hand, are sold at considerably higher prices, many in multiples of thousands of yen. Even then, many need financial subvention to meet the cost of publication, such as that provided by the Ministry of Education, Culture, and Science.

To appeal to the mass, a product must have attractive packaging and lots of publicity. Paperbacks intended for the mass market have attractive covers even if illustrations inside are mostly in black and white – or eliminated entirely to cut the cost. Such books are often advertised in newspapers having national circulation and also in popular magazines with circulations in tens or hundreds of thousands – the sort of publicity scholarly books would not receive, not only because the meager sales would not justify such expensive advertisement but also because such books are not intended for the mass.

Publishers and writers of *Nihonjinron* are producers of consumer goods; readers are the consumers. The relationship between the two is asymmetrical. Consumers might complain to producers or to an appropriate authority about products that are seriously defective or dangerous to life or health, but they generally do not engage in debate with the producer about how good the product is or where the product may be improved. Popular *Nihonjinron* writers deliver products to be consumed by readers. This is totally unlike the relationship among scholars who engage in scholarly discourse, where both writers (producers) and readers (consumers) are peers who exchange their views and ideas. People who are writers (producers) at one time are readers (consumers) at another, and vice versa. Scholars, writers and readers alike, engage in mutual discourse about their products (writings), such discussion being the stuff of scholarship.

Some types of consumer goods improve in quality, and consumers then are moved to buy superior products. Technological improvements have created better computers, better automobiles, better tape-recorders, better cameras, and better television sets. Improvements are obvious, and consumers all want to buy better products. In the same fashion, genuine scholarship is dependent on accumulation of data, quality of data, refinements in analytical tools such as concepts and theories, and improvements in methodology. Arguments in scholarly *Nihonjinron* thus improve with time.

Other types of consumer goods, however, do not necessarily improve in quality – instead, they change with fashion, as clothing does. Consumers are moved to buy the latest in fashion, simply because that is what everyone prefers. In the same fashion, so to speak, the popular *Nihonjinron* industry is also very much determined by market needs and demands. The fashion in popular *Nihonjinron*, like fashion in apparel, changes from time to time without qualitative improvement in the argument. I will argue in Chapter Seven that geoeconomic and geopolitical processes produce the kind of *Nihonjinron* desired and fashionable in a given historical period.

## Commodification

Since the mass seek in *Nihonjinron* self-identity in cultural context, the task of publishers and *Nihonjinron* writers as producers of consumer goods is to provide merchandise that satisfies consumers. Setting aside the question of what kind of self-identity appeals to consumers, the process is like an artist painting the portrait of a client. The consumer is more likely to be willing to pay for a portrait that flatters the subject, not one that reveals every detail – moles, wrinkles, and all. 'Artistic license' may have to be exercised to tickle the consumer into liking the product. Even a portrait photographer can and does doctor a portrait, touching up the negative here and there to make the image look more beautiful or more handsome than the real person. A portrait painter has even greater license, as brushes are not subject to the kind of accuracy the lens of a camera is stuck with.

In terms of the extent of freedom allowed in creating the portrait of 'the Japanese' or 'the Japanese culture,' writing *Nihonjinron* is more like painting a portrait than taking a photograph. Slight distortions of facts, along with stretching of imagination and emphasis (read exaggeration) of certain facts, are a literary license *Nihonjinron* writers engage in to create the kind of 'self-portrait' that appeals to the public, the kind that sells. Cultural homogeneity, groupism, harmony, unspoken or nonverbal communication, love of nature, and the like are some of the clichés we encounter regularly in *Nihonjinron* literature. Conflict in Japan, as in hundreds of peasant uprisings in recent history? No. Verboseness, as in the immensely popular sitcom *manzai*? No. Individuals who act like lone wolves, such as the Meiji period populist Tanaka Shōzō? No. These patterns of Japanese culture, though solidly documented, do not appeal to the public or cajole the mass; hence they are omitted.

Most people nowadays cannot sew their own clothes, at least to their satisfaction. They end up buying ready-made clothes at a store, trying on various items to see which fashion suits them best. *Nihonjinron* is like ready-made clothing. Most people do not have the competence or time to write or formulate their own *Nihonjinron*, so they buy a book that suits them – one that fits their taste or their own vision of what they think the cultural identity of the Japanese is. *Nihonjinron* writers have provided the public with hundreds of ready-made cultural portraits from which to pick and choose. Writers must write and provide what the consumer needs; otherwise their books would not sell.

In this brief consideration, I have argued that popular *Nihonjinron* is best understood as mass-produced consumer goods, rather than as serious scholarship, and that by seeing it thus, we go a long way in understanding the phenomenon. In doing so, we need to understand how popular in fact popular *Nihonjinron* is. An important caveat is in order. Popularity of *Nihonjinron* as evidenced in sales figures of books in this genre is not to be immediately understood to mean that readers believe everything they read. A Japanese may buy a book to learn about a subject without accepting the author's arguments. We shall see in the next chapter the distinction between believing in the propositions of *Nihonjinron* and just being curious about them.

# 4  Premises, Models, and Ideologies

The nature and formation of cultural and national identity, though seemingly simple and straightforward, are complex issues. This chapter examines the assumptions, premises, and methodology of *Nihonjinron*. We shall also look into the anthropological concept of 'cultural model' and regard *Nihonjinron* as a species of cultural model. We shall argue that Nihonjinron as a cultural model is ideologically hegemonic – that is, it is normatively all-encompassing, and with official sponsorship, attempts to control rather than merely describe reality – and thus has policy implications.

## Uniqueness of the Japanese

Belief in the uniqueness of the Japanese people is a salient and pervasive feature of 'Japanese mentality' and is the foundation of *Nihonjinron*. It is a truism that every culture is in some sense unique. However, to what extent participants of a culture are conscious of or insistent on this uniqueness is an empirical question. Americans, for example, are not much concerned with the uniqueness of their culture, at least not to the extent that the Japanese are. For the Japanese, their own uniqueness and that of the Japanese culture figure prominently in their conscious thinking. When they characterize their ethnic identity and origin, they are most likely to do this by emphasizing the uniqueness of Japanese culture or of some features of it, be they group orientation, hierarchy, harmony, or *amae*, as discussed in Chapter Two. Some of these may indeed be unique, but others have a dubious claim to uniqueness in the world inasmuch as most such claims are based on comparison of Japanese culture only with the West, mainly the United States, or no comparison at all. Some supposedly unique features, such as hierarchy, may well be shared with Korea or China, Japan's neighbors, about whom most Japanese know surprisingly little, or with one culture or another of areas farther afield, such as Southeast Asia or Africa. But the truth of the claimed uniqueness of certain Japanese cultural features is not in question; what is at issue is the invincible *belief in* that uniqueness and the claiming of uniqueness in the *Nihonjinron* discourse.

This notion of uniqueness is often accompanied by a belief that these unique features cannot be understood or fully comprehended by non-Japanese. Comprehension of these unique features supposedly requires not rational or logical understanding but an intuitive insight into Japanese culture that only natives can achieve. Thus foreigners are defined as incapable of understanding the essence of Japanese culture. This belief gives comfort to the Japanese: here is one essential 'sociocultural territory' they can protect as their own. The notion that foreigners could fully comprehend Japanese culture and therefore act and behave like any Japanese threatens their ethnic and national integrity.

The claim of uniqueness is argued from a particularistic point of view. The Japanese language itself offers another convenient tactic, because Japanese believe that their language is spoken natively only by themselves. Of course, each language of the world is unique in exactly the same sense, but that argument does not destroy the uniqueness of Japanese – hence the plethora of writings on the Japanese language as a demonstration of Japanese uniqueness. Inasmuch as the language is unique, cultural meanings derived from it are also ipso facto unique, so the argument goes. The uniqueness of Japanese culture is thus readily established.

## Ethnocentrism

Founded as *Nihonjinron* is on uniqueness, an inherent ethnocentrism is one salient property of contemporary writings in the genre. *Nihonjinron* is formulated by comparing Japan with other cultures to arrive at what is presumably unique to Japan. But this comparison is not objective, as one can surmise from the value judgment, either explicit or implicit, accompanying *Nihonjinron* propositions. Praising one's own culture need not lead automatically to disparaging other cultures compared with it. Valuative comparisons are, however, quite common in *Nihonjinron*, where Japanese culture is not only good in itself but better (or worse, as the case may be) than other cultures. In the wake of Japan's unprecedented economic success from the 1960s through the 1980s, the Japanese are all the more inclined to congratulate themselves and disparage others, for they base this success on certain unique cultural features such as those propounded in *Nihonjinron*.

Some of the worst culprits of this ethnocentrism are business expatriates stationed abroad, who readily disparage locals for everything that is not like Japan. Their logic is simple: Japan became an economic giant because of what Japan is; therefore, whatever is not Japanese-like in the local culture is the reason for the economic backwardness of the country of assignment (Ben-Ari 2000).

Higuchi Kiyoyuki, whose *Nihonjinron* writings unabashedly congratulate the Japanese for how smart, how creative, and how ingenious they are, perhaps best epitomizes this contemporary trend. Higuchi continues to write in this vein with unrelenting zeal, breaking his own publication record almost every year. As of 2000, he had more than 120 books to his credit. In one of his earlier works (Higuchi 1974b), for example, Higuchi sees the genius of Japanese culture in the invention of the dried and marinated plum called *umeboshi*, which is supposed to be a cure-all folk medicine and health food. He also sees the Japanese metallurgical genius in the technology of the Japanese sword. Along the same line, Nakagawa (1978, English version 1979) argues that Japan is a 'welfare superstate' and a paradise for workers, far surpassing Western countries.

## Premises of *Nihonjinron*

Nihonjinron argument is premised on the assumption that the Japanese people are a homogeneous 'race' and possess a homogeneous culture, whatever the term may mean and whatever the contents of homogeneity might be. It also implicitly assumes equivalence of land, race, language, and culture.

### Homogeneity

One of the major premises on which the uniqueness thesis rests is the assumption that Japan is culturally homogeneous (*tōshitsu* or *dōshitsu*). Anthropologist Ishida Eiichirō (1969: 154) has observed that Japan maintains 'amazing homogeneity' in comparison with European cultures. More recently Oguma Eiji (1995), in his award-winning book, has given us an intellectual genealogy of the origin and development of the homogeneity thesis, namely that the Japanese nation is made up of an ethnic group sharing the same language and culture and that the Japanese archipelago has been inhabited from ancient times by a genetically homogeneous race.

According to linguist Suzuki Takao (1980) of Keio University, Japan's homogeneity has several components. The first is racial homogeneity, which he qualifies as 'perceived homogeneity,' that is, a belief in homogeneity, regardless of how heterogeneous the reality of Japanese racial makeup may be. This acknowledgment that ultimately *Nihonjinron* has to do with perception and belief, or 'cultural construction,' is important to keep in mind. And the cultural construction of homogeneity keeps on living in Japan in face of the reality of multicultural heterogeneity, as has been argued by such prominent scholars as Amino (1982), Fukuoka (1993), and Ōnuma (1986). (See also Denoon ed. 1996; Weiner 1997.)

Suzuki's approach to this multicultural reality is typical. He does not consider the heterogeneous elements in Japan to pose a problem for the homogeneity thesis. He considers the Ainu population too small – indeed there probably are no more than a few thousand pure Ainu left – to be of any consequence. He does not believe that Koreans constitute a problem, either, because the majority of Koreans are culturally and linguistically so assimilated as to be indistinguishable from Japanese. This summary dismissal of ethnic minorities in Japan is an explicit stance, a conscious decision made by *Nihonjinron* writers like Suzuki to ignore ethnic heterogeneity in Japan. In short, racial and ethnic homogeneity in Japan is not an objective fact, it is instead a construct of those who are motivated to promote a certain cultural conception of Japan.

Suzuki also refers to homogeneity in language, religion, and lifestyle. This assumption of homogeneity is important because it enables *Nihonjinron* authors to apply generalizations across the board to all Japanese. It assumes that local, class, gender, and other variations within Japan are not important enough to violate the essential sameness throughout Japanese culture and among all Japanese.

This is not to say that the Japanese are not aware of internal variations or that research on these variations is lacking. Popular accounts abound about stereotypical differences among Japanese of different regions, occupations, classes, and the like. Tokyoites are supposed to be spendthrift: the saying *Edokko wa yoigoshi no kane o motazu* (Tokyoites don't hold on to money overnight; they spend it all the day they earn it) is cited as proof of uniqueness of Tokyoites. People in the merchant city of Osaka are supposedly obsessed with making money and eating gourmet food. Kyoto people, besides being obsessed with possessing beautiful clothes, are self-designated aristocrats who look down on all others, especially Tokyoites, as country bumpkins.

To establish objective bases of claims of regional variation, numerous research projects have been carried out on the 'character' of people of different regions (for example, NHK Hōsō Yoron Chōsajo ed. 1979). Anthropologist Sofue Takao (1971, 2000) has also written on the 'prefectural character (*kenminsei*)' of the Japanese. These attitude surveys indicate the extent to which perception of regional differences is alive among Japanese.

We are familiar with regional differences in social organization in traditional Japan through works of generations of scholars. A half-century ago Izumi and Gamō (1952) published their compilation of regional variations, combed from ethnographic reports from all over Japan. Their findings were updated by a more comprehensive nationwide questionnaire survey on social and cultural practices (Nagashima 1964; Nagashima and Tomoeda ed. 1984). These and other studies show marked contrasts between the so-called northeastern (or *dōzoku*) type of village structure and the southwestern (or *kōgumi*) type, where the former emphasizes hierarchy and the latter horizontal ties among households. The age-grade system, where villagers were organized into several groups of similar ages, was strong in southern coastal areas but was absent in northern Japan. Whether it be beliefs in spirit possession practices or burial of the dead, mode of traditional transportation, type of house, or fishing and agricultural technology, regional variations are legion in Japan.

While these academic studies do demonstrate regional variations within Japan beyond doubt, they are scholarly findings. To demonstrate awareness of regional variation among ordinary people, Kazufumi Manabe and I included questions on this topic in the 1987 Nishinomiya survey (Befu and Manabe

1989, 1991). Results showed that the majority of respondents were well aware of internal variations in the Japanese population not only regionally but in terms of age, sex, generation, rurality-urbanity, dialect, income, politics, occupation, and education. Only a small proportion – between 8 percent and 24 percent – did not recognize internal variations.

The neglect of internal variations along class, gender, region, and the like in favor of espousing the homogeneity thesis manifested in *Nihonjinron* is, therefore, not due to lack of information or awareness. Instead, it is based on a conscious decision on the part of *Nihonjinron* writers to represent a homogeneous stance with respect to Japanese culture.

## Land = People = Culture = Language

The second assumption behind *Nihonjinron* asserts the co-terminousness of geography, race, language, and culture, a point made explicit recently by Sugimoto (1999). This is a set of interrelated propositions:

- Japanese culture, its 'carrier,' and native speakers of Japanese alike exist coterminously with the Japanese archipelago, extending throughout the islands but not beyond its bounds, with minor exceptions such as recent immigrants to North and South America.
- All those practicing Japanese culture but no others speak the Japanese language natively, and all native speakers of Japanese are practitioners of Japanese culture.
- Carriers of Japanese culture and therefore speakers of the Japanese language all share 'blood' and have done so for thousands of years.
- No significant amount of new blood has been infused into this allegedly pure Japanese race.

In short, a claim is made for equivalency and mutual implications among land, people (that is, race), culture, and language, such that those and only those who practice the culture also speak the language and have inherited Japanese 'blood' from their forebears, who have always lived on the Japanese archipelago, and that no other person speaks the language natively and practices the culture.

The implicit genetic determinism mentioned earlier assumes that cultural and linguistic competencies inhere in the genes ('blood') of the Japanese. Since only those with Japanese genes are capable of practicing Japanese culture and speaking Japanese, mutatis mutandis no foreigner, with exceptions so rare as to make no difference, is supposedly capable of full competence in Japanese (Miller 1982, chap. 8).

This implicit genetic determinism is manifested in a curious way. When third- and fourth-generation American-born Japanese – *sansei* and *yonsei* – travel to Japan without any proficiency in the language, the Japanese are extremely curious as to why a person with a Japanese surname and Japanese physical appearance is unable to speak Japanese and think and act like other Japanese (T. Suzuki 1980: 363). When these Japanese Americans and Japanese Latins do learn the language, Japanese are short of praise, as if learning the language (which is 'in the genes,' as it were) should be the most natural thing, whereas Caucasians who learn a few words of Japanese are considered to have accomplished a major feat worthy of high praise.

## Methodology

What is the methodology of *Nihonjinron*, if there is any, beyond reliance on intuition and experience? One of the common ways to discover one's identity – whether individual identity or group identity – is to compare oneself with others. Ethnic identity is typically constructed by making such comparisons and then emphasizing either real or imaginary differences from other ethnic groups or supposedly unique characteristics. *Nihonjinron* writers follow this prescription from the most explicit comparison to the most implicit. An author might comment, for example, that only in Japan would one find certain cultural traits, linguistic features, or personality characteristics – without ever bothering to demonstrate their absence in other cultures.

Implicit comparison is illustrated in the works of Higuchi, who, for example, boasts the wisdom of the ancestors of the Japanese for selecting zelkova (*keyaki*) as windbreaks around a house in northern Japan (1974a: 12–14) because zelkova is deciduous, shedding its leaves in winter, when one wants maximum sunlight in and on the house. Here, comparison is only implicit. But it is there; otherwise Higuchi has no reason to boast of this supposedly unique Japanese practice. He is implying that this wisdom is not seen in the rest of the world.

Generally speaking, comparisons are implicit when the *Nihonjinron* propositions to be adduced are those that are already salient in Japanese culture as *emic* concepts, that is, as functional elements of the system recognized by members of the culture. For example, Minamoto (1969) devotes a whole volume to the concepts of *on* (social indebtedness) and *giri* (obligation to reciprocate), without so much as referring to similar concepts or their functional equivalents in other cultures. For those *etic* – that is, observed by outsiders – propositions for which ready emic concepts are not available, however, comparison becomes an important tool for eliciting propositions in *Nihonjinron*. The notion of Japanese group orientation is an apt example here. It is primarily through comparison of Japanese behavior against Western individualism that the idea of Japanese groupism has been derived.

At the explicit end of the continuum, I cite *Nihonjin to Yudayajin* (The Japanese and the Jews) by Isaiah BenDasan (1970), a best-seller among all *Nihonjinron* best-sellers along with Ruth Benedict's *Kiku to Katana* (1948 and later editions), the Japanese translation of *The Chrysanthemum and the Sword* (1946). BenDasan, about whom we shall have more to say in Chapter Six, compares the Japanese with the Jews with respect to attitudes, values, dispositions, and the like toward nature, society, law, and so on. The Japanese, for example, living as they do in a monsoon zone, supposedly think water is free, whereas the Jews, living in desert, never take water for granted. One reader might think this sort of comparison cavalier, but another might praise it for its insight. Some books offer comparisons with respect to a specific aspect or feature of culture. For example, Suzuki Hideo (1978) argues that Japanese and Europeans think differently because Japanese culture arose in a 'forest' setting, and European culture in a 'desert' setting. Similarly Sabata Toyoyuki (1979) assumes that different dietary practices – meat-eating versus rice-eating – are emblematic of different ways of thinking and different sets of values. Similarly, Hisaeda Kohei (1976) observes that a culture in which an explicit written contract is the norm differs significantly from the kind of culture in which implicit understanding serves for a contract.

Most such cross-cultural comparisons are with the West or a subset thereof. Among all comparisons, that of Japan with the United States is the most popular – because of the long and intense relationship between the two countries since the end of World War II certainly, but also because of even longer antecedents going back to the middle of the nineteenth century. Psychologist Miyagi Otoya (1976), comparing 'the American personality' with 'the Japanese personality,' offers one among numerous comparisons of the Japanese with Americans. A similar but more general essay is Kamei Shunsuke's comparison of 'America's heart' with 'Japan's heart' (1975). Kimata Shin'ichi and Kimata Mitsu's comparison refers to Japan and the United States as 'warm' and 'cold' societies (1973). Other comparisons with the West include Masuzoe Yōichi's comparison of the Japanese with the French (1982), Matsubara Hisako's 'Japan's wisdom' with 'Europe's wisdom' (1985), and economist Morishima Michio's numerous comparisons of Japan with England (1977, 1978). Some cross-cultural comparisons are with Asian cultures, such as Nakamura's (1948–49, 1965 for English translation), but they are very rare.[15]

Among explicit comparisons, a favorite pastime for *Nihonjinron* writers is to regard Japan as an 'agricultural' society and contrast it with the West (Araki 1973: 23–25; Fukasaku 1971: 65–70; Iwasaki 1980: 34; Kenmochi 1980: 75, 137–149; Okada 1972: 21–28; Watanabe 1975; Watsuji 1935). Never mind that in the last several decades less than 10 percent of the Japanese workforce has been engaged full time in agriculture; the legacy of Japan's agricultural past is assumed to dominate its contemporary culture. In this comparison, the West is turned into a horseback riders' society by Watanabe (1975),[16] a pastoralist society by Araki (1973) and Watsuji (1935), and a hunting society by Okada (1972). Watanabe's 'agricultural' type, to which Japan belongs, is basically what most other *Nihonjin* writers call 'the group-oriented type' of society in reference to Japan. In this type of society, emphasis is placed on seniority and harmony with neighbors. The 'horseback-rider type' of state, on the other hand, is supposedly characterized by bureaucratic efficiency.[17]

## Racial Hierarchy

When Japan entered the period of massive borrowing of cultural elements from China in the sixth and seventh centuries C.E., China had far more advanced technology and political and religious institutions, and was the only center of civilization known to Japan. Twelve centuries later, Japan was made aware of the military might and the technological superiority of the West, and went through another period of massive borrowing, this time from Europe and the United States.

Such borrowings indicate not only the intense curiosity of the Japanese but also their feeling of inferiority to the West and their unswerving disposition to regard the West as their mentor. At the base of this feeling of inferiority toward the West and toward white men and women was the technological, military, and economic inferiority of the Japanese civilization, which, however, extended into the whole social and cultural inventory. If the Japanese felt lower than Westerners who happened to be white, by the same token, they felt superior toward the peoples of Southeast Asia and Africa, whose technological level is below Japan's and who are not white. In short, the cultural as well as 'racial' hierarchy has placed the West above Japan, and Africa and the rest of Asia below it.

This prejudice against peoples of less developed countries smacks of racism. We have seen this racism in another guise, namely in the assumption of genetic inheritance of culture. Racial minorities do not loom large in Japan in terms of numbers. Blacks are all but nonexistent. So are South and Southeast Asians, although in recent years increasing numbers have entered Japan, legally and illegally, to work. Blacks, of course, are obviously non-Japanese, and people from South and Southeast Asia are generally distinguishable from Japanese by physical traits. Those groups, therefore, are subject to blatant discrimination. Because the large numbers of Koreans and Chinese who live in Japan are racially indistinguishable from Japanese, the prejudicial attitude Japanese have toward them is more a case of ethnic prejudice and discrimination, that is, ethnocentrism, rather than racial prejudice, although in conceptual terms it is difficult to distinguish between 'race' and 'ethnicity' in Japanese discourse. Caucasians who live in Japan represent the dominant West and constitute an economically powerful group. As such they are not discriminated against in the way Asians and Africans are – although to be sure, they are excluded from full participation in Japanese society simply by virtue of their foreignness.

It is interesting in considering Japanese attitudes toward foreigners that the term *gaijin* has dual meanings. In the generic sense, it refers to all foreigners; but in a more restricted sense it designates only Caucasians – that is, those foreigners who are worthy of admiration in some respects. It is this racial and ethnic hierarchy, then, that defines the shape of *Nihonjinron* argument.

## Cultural Model

A number of anthropologists have conceptualized culture as a model of some sort. Geertz (1973) has called it a 'cultural system.' One might call it a 'folk model' (Holy and Stuchlik 1981) or a 'world view' (Kearney 1984). I do not for a moment imply that these different conceptions are all the same. Grouping them together simply has the heuristic value of recognizing a common endeavor among anthropologists to understand the relevance of the native's thinking in deciphering cultural codes. *Nihonjinron* is a system of knowledge of the sort that anthropologists endeavor to understand.

Folk knowledge is necessarily unevenly distributed in a population (Holy and Stuchlik 1981: 18). With reference specifically to *Nihonjinron*, this means that some Japanese are more interested in and knowledgeable about Japan's cultural identity than others and that different Japanese have different notions about the subject matter. Some Japanese are producers of books on the subject, some are avid readers, and others take little or no interest.

In the 1987 Nishinomiya survey, 82 percent of those asked said that they were interested in the subject in varying degrees; 13 percent indicated lack of interest and 5 percent did not respond to this inquiry. Those taking 'a great deal of interest' are presumably on the whole more knowledgeable and more able to articulate views on the subject. Their *Nihonjinron* model is more comprehensive than that of those taking little or no interest. It is important to keep this individual variation in mind lest we end up with the essentialized caricature of 'all Japanese doing the same thing.' Items of knowledge are differently distributed and combined into variant models that differ from one another (Holy and Stuchlik 1981: 81). Thus *Nihonjinron* as a cultural model is expected to vary from one Japanese to another. It should be clear that when we speak of *Nihonjinron* as a folk model, we are implying that it does not represent the totality of Japanese culture, which encompasses far wider ranges of phenomena.

The ground in which *Nihonjinron* grows is, of course, one's lifelong enculturation process as a Japanese. This experiential knowledge serves as the context in which the more articulated variety of *Nihonjinron* is received, and a 'personalized' *Nihonjinron* is thus formulated. Which sources a given individual uses to construct this personal model most certainly varies from one individual to another. Thus it is safe to say that no two individual Japanese possess precisely the same stock of knowledge about Japan and thus precisely the same model about Japanese culture.

Moreover, a given person's *Nihonjinron* model is not a static one, but is constantly changing in a sort of feedback loop, being revised over and over as the person's experience increases, and with exposure to more *Nihonjinron* literature or new situations relevant to the formulation of *Nihonjinron*. For example, a Japanese might travel to North or South America and encounter third- or fourth-generation Japanese who, though genetically 'pure' representatives of the people, are unable to speak any of the language. This experience may force the traveler to abandon the tenet of *Nihonjinron* that claims proficiency in Japanese to be genetically based.

Here we need to distinguish between what Levi-Strauss calls 'conscious' and 'unconscious' models (Levi-Strauss 1953: 526–527). *Nihonjinron* as formulated by writers of the subject is a conscious model. On the other hand, models held by ordinary Japanese who might think about the issue only occasionally and who are not able to articulate their thoughts are unconscious or semiconscious in the sense that these Japanese are not able to describe all or even most facets of *Nihonjinron*. But how much a given Japanese can articulate the model is a matter of degree. To that extent, conscious and unconscious models of *Nihonjinron* are extremes of a continuum rather than dichotomous categories.

In the conception adopted here, a cultural model is in the head of each native, and therefore there are as many folk models as there are natives. Each Japanese has some conception about Japanese cultural identity. This individuality of concept does not preclude the possibility of sharing of knowledge. Indeed, without at least some sharing, without some agreement on rules of conduct, cultural values, and disposition of one's affect, social life would be impossible. Thus individual *Nihonjinron* models must overlap to a greater or lesser degree.

When we speak of *Nihonjinron*, we are necessarily hedging the issue of 'which one?' or 'whose?' We cannot, for practical reasons, refer to every single *Nihonjinron* model carried in the head of each Japanese. We assume that the literature on *Nihonjinron* represents folk models of a significant portion of the population.

This multiplicity of models is demonstrated in the Nishinomiya survey. How important 'blood' is for defining the Japanese, to what extent foreigners may participate in Japanese society, what besides 'blood' defines Japaneseness – for all these questions and many others having to do with essential qualities of Japaneseness and Japanese culture, responses varied widely, demonstrating that each respondent carries a unique model of Japanese culture, society, and people.

## Prescriptive Model

On its face, *Nihonjinron* seems to be a purely descriptive cultural model, describing, however faulty it might be, how Japanese culture is, as conceived in the minds of those who propound *Nihonjinron*. It is well to remember, however, that a declarative statement in Japanese, as in European languages, often carries normative implications when put in idealized form – as *Nihonjinron* propositions generally are. To take a few examples at random, Japanese are said to achieve harmony by belonging to a hierarchically organized group in which human relations are based on particularism, functional diffuseness, and trust, as expounded by *Nihonjinron* protagonists like Nakane Chie (1970). Doi (1973) describes how Japanese thrive on the affective diet of *amae*. Kyōgoku (1983: 251–253) tells us that Japanese politicians deal with their constituencies with parental thoughtfulness. Tsuda (1977: 206–207) describes the Japanese labor union in terms of 'enterprise unionism,' where all workers of a given company, no matter what their occupational specialty, belong to one union.

Note that these are all declarative, not imperative, statements. They are supposedly statements of observed facts, that is, they are descriptive models. But these descriptive models at the same time characterize an idealized, desirable state of affairs and carry positive valence. Hence it behooves Japanese to act and think as described so as to achieve the idealized condition, that is, to treat the descriptive model as a prescriptive model. In short, the *is* in *Nihonjinron* propositions is read as *should*. Declarative propositions become moral imperatives. Not to behave as prescribed is not only unusual and strange, it is regarded as 'un-Japanese' and against normative standards of the society. Only a thin line here separates a descriptive model from a normative model, as normative elements are deceptively disguised in the declarative and seemingly descriptive statements of the cultural model. It is probably all the more effective, though perhaps more insidious, to slip imperative implications into descriptive statements. In this way, people are led, or subliminally misled as the case may be, from approval of a descriptive model to espousal of imperative commands. *Nihonjinron* as a *description of* behavior thus becomes a *model for* behavior.

There is another insidious and covert way in which *Nihonjinron* serves as a moral imperative. Propositions of *Nihonjinron* are often stated in universal terms, or at least imply that all normal Japanese behave in the ways claimed in *Nihonjinron*. However, our survey data from Nishinomiya demonstrate that a significant minority, and sometimes even a majority, disclaim espousal of one or another *Nihonjinron* proposition. For example, only 35.7 percent of the sample 'strongly' or 'somewhat' support the claim that no foreigner can master the Japanese language.

Yet the unconditional, universal mode of *Nihonjinron* claims seemingly implies, whether true or not, that *all* Japanese subscribe to *Nihonjinron* propositions. To be counted as true Japanese, then, many Japanese feel compelled, in varying degrees, to practice what is prescribed. To make this prescription even more compelling, moreover, claims contradicting *Nihonjinron* propositions, such as regarding foreigners' linguistic competence, are seldom if ever voiced. If a foreigner is found to be totally fluent in Japanese, the case is usually dismissed as an exception to the rule.

*Nihonjinron* as a moral prescription seems to have effectively silenced contrary views and alternative models, as will be taken up in later chapters.

Intellectual hegemony thus is an important dimension of the imperative nature of *Nihonjinron*. One might say that *Nihonjinron* writings serve as a modern moral textbook, all the more effective because they are not the ordinary textbooks used in classrooms and didactically taught to students. If they were literally school texts, as *shushin* (morals) texts were before and during World War II, they would be scrutinized and surely criticized by any number of organizations that are serving as watchdogs of the educational system. Instead, *Nihonjinron* is promoted as source material for Japanese cultural and national identity – that is, as knowledge any intelligent Japanese should possess.

In the private sector, endorsement of various *Nihonjinron* propositions (especially those dealing with group orientation and interpersonal harmony) by the business establishment is widespread, as Yoshino (1992) has observed. One sees this in the New Year's statements made by corporate executives, speeches by company presidents at the induction ceremonies of new recruits in April, and in company mottoes, usually called *shakun* or *shaze*. These and many other means of moral exhortation emphasize cooperation and harmony among workers, loyalty to the company, hard work and dedication, contribution to the society through the workplace, and similar values – all of which are tenets derivable from *Nihonjinron*.

## Cultural Policy

It is only a short step from *Nihonjinron* as a prescriptive model to *Nihonjinron* as an ideology. It is highly instructive, in this regard, to analyze the report submitted to Prime Minister Ōhira Masayoshi. This report, titled *Bunka no Jidai* (The Age of Culture) (Bunka no Jidai Kenkyū Gurūpu 1980), is subtitled 'Reports of the Policy Group of Prime Minister Ōhira – Number One.' It was prepared by a committee of *Nihonjinron* advocates appointed by Ōhira. The committee was chaired by Yamamoto Shichihei, also known as Isaiah BenDasan, author of the three-million-copy best-seller, *Nihonjin to Yudayajin* (1970), and included a number of other well-known *Nihonjinron* writers, such as the Tokyo University professor Kumon Shumpei, one of the co-authors, along with two other Tokyo University professors, of an erudite *Nihonjinron* treatise (Murakami, Kumon, and Satō 1979), that argues for the familistic basis of Japanese society. Another notable member of the committee was Komatsu Sakyō, one of the best-known science fiction and mystery writers and author of another *Nihonjinron* piece (1977).

The committee report hails Japanese culture for its emphasis on harmonious human relations – contrasting such relations with the self-centered individualism of the West – on members of society knowing their station in life, and on Japanese tradition in general. For the first time after the war, Kawamura (1982: chap. 4) observes, *Nihonjinron* thus formally entered politics and became a handmaiden of the political establishment, which saw fit to endorse *Nihonjinron* as an officially sanctioned and thus hegemonic ideology.

It is no surprise, then, to find the Department of Comprehensive Policy Studies of Chūō University adopting analysis of *Nihonjinron* as a major approach to formulation of comprehensive national policy. Moreover, the department organized a two-year graduate seminar on *Nihonjinron*, with the participation of some twenty-five faculty members, the results of which were published in 2000 (Chūō Daigaku Daigakuin Sōgō Seisaku Kenkyūka Nihonron Iinkai ed. 2000)

Thus intellectuals write *Nihonjinron* as prescription for behavior. The government turns it into a hegemonic ideology, and the corporate establishment puts it into practice.

It should come as no surprise that the hegemonic ideology of *Nihonjinron* is maintained and supported by the state in many and varied forms. The government's annual award of cultural medals to those who excel in traditional artistic fields is one. Governmental designation of an artist as a 'Human Cultural Treasure' is another. These medals and designations are given out to only a handful of individuals each year. Because they are given in fields of traditional arts and crafts, these awards indicate state endorsement of traditional Japanese esthetic values incorporated in *Nihonjinron*, such as *yūgen*, *wabi*, and *sabi*.

National monuments often serve to reinforce the sense of cultural and national identity, as these monuments often attempt to assert a sense of cultural uniqueness. Among such monuments, I might mention state-run museums. The Historical and Folklore

Museum (Rekishi Minzoku Hakubutsukan), exhibiting the essence of Japanese history, is a veritable showcase of cultural nationalism. The National Museums of Art, in Tokyo and Kyoto, accomplish the same objective, namely, to impress upon visitors that which is unique to Japanese culture and history – the very essence of *Nihonjinron*. These museums help to assert Japan's unique identity by housing artifacts unique to Japan.

The Japanese government has taken upon itself the task of promoting and propagating the official *Nihonjinron* overseas. This overseas propagation of *Nihonjinron* should be seen as an integral part of the *Nihonjinron* phenomenon, for it is in large part because of Japan's internationalization and globalization that *Nihonjinron* has become a burning issue among Japanese. I have explicated earlier (1983) the relationship between *Nihonjinron* and Japan's internationalization. Briefly, as Japan internationalizes, accepting foreigners and adapting foreign culture to Japanese soil on one hand and going abroad and spreading Japanese economic tentacles overseas on the other, the Japanese increasingly confront cultures different from their own and thus become aware of the need to define themselves and their culture in a process now known as 'glocalization.' I have long pointed out that *Nihonjinron* fulfills this need (Befu 1983). But this self-definition serves as a self-definition only when it is accepted by outsiders. It is for this reason that the Japanese government expends so much energy on propagating *Nihonjinron* abroad.

This takes the form, for example, of the government's financing English translation and publication of some of the *Nihonjinron* classics, as pointed out by Mouer and Sugimoto (1986: 177–178). Nakamura Hajime's *The Way of Thinking of Eastern Peoples* (1965) and Watsuji Tetsurō's *A Climate* (1961) are results of such government effort. This effort reached a new, heightened level when the Japanese government took it upon itself to print Nakane Chie's *Human Relations in Japan* (1972), a government version, as it were, of her *Japanese Society* (1970), and distributed thousands of copies free of charge throughout the world through its embassies and consulates.

The Japan Foundation, established during the term of Premier Tanaka Kakuei, has done perhaps more than any other single government agency in disseminating the tenets and premises of

*Nihonjinron* throughout the world. From its inception, it has sent scholars abroad to show how unique Japan is, has sent artists of traditional Japanese art forms such as kabuki, noh, bunraku, and calligraphy – all of which, needless to say, demonstrated the unique essence of Japanese culture.

More recently, in 1988 an International Center for Japanese Studies was established by the government as a result of Prime Minister Nakasone's interest in promoting cooperative inter-national research on Japanese culture. As soon as the center came into being, it was widely rumored, without any evidence, that its covert mission was to formulate, validate, and disseminate *Nihonjinron*. What made this suspicion plausible to many is that Nakasone is regarded as a nationalist, having credited Japan's supposed ethnic homogeneity for its economic success, and that Umehara Takeshi, the center's founding director-general, himself is an active player in the *Nihonjinron* game.

## Primordiality and Civic Sentiment

It was Clifford Geertz who in 1963 explored the implications of the primordial definition of ethnicity in the formation of the state in developing countries (Geertz 1963). *Primordiality* of an ethnic group has to do with the symbolic importance of language, religion, sense of 'community,' the notion of 'shared blood,' and the idea of 'common history' and 'shared tradition' in defining the ethnic group and establishing the identity of its members. Benedict Anderson (1983) argued the importance of language in the formation of nationalism, in creating – along with what he ingeniously called 'print capitalism' – a sense of 'community' among those who speak the same language and read the same print. This sense of community promotes exclusiveness when the language is spoken natively only by the ethnic group. Japanese is a case in point. It – like Danish, Finnish, Korean, and Thai – is spoken natively only within the boundary of the nation and by those native to the country. English, in contrast, is spoken by peoples of many lands, nations, and cultures. English thus does not aid in fomenting nationalism.

The importance of language in creating an identity stems not only from the fact of speaking a common tongue, but as we saw, also from the unique semiotic domain implied in the language. What can be said about language in relation to ethnic identity can be repeated for religion. A religion that is unique to a given ethnic group can help define the identity of the group in a way a religion such as Christianity or Islam would have difficulty doing. It would be difficult, for example, for the French to use Catholicism as a basis of defining French uniqueness.

In contrast, all Japanese have to do is to point to Shintoism as an attribute of Japan's uniqueness, because Shintoism is a unique, indigenous religion. By elevating it from folk belief to the state religion and placing the emperor as its centerpiece, the Japanese state created a unique religious basis for its nationalism.[18]

Most modern nation-states consist of multiple ethnic groups. This is true of the United States, the United Kingdom, Western European nations, and most postcolonial states. It is also true of Japan, despite the claim of cultural and ethnic homogeneity by *Nihonjinron* protagonists. For Japan has nearly three-quarters of a million Koreans living within its boundaries. The Ainu, though small in numbers, are conspicuous as an ethnic minority because of their distinct culture (Denoon ed. 1996). Chinese, South and Southeast Asians, Latin Americans, and Europeans also are present in increasing numbers (Weiner ed. 1997). Japanese culture and society are what they are today precisely because of contributions made by all those who are not ethnic Japanese. Without their contributions to the current state of Japan's economy, Japanese culture and society would not be what they are.

Herein lies the difficulty of basing Japan's national identity on the primordial homogeneity of the ethnic Japanese: such an identity automatically excludes other ethnic groups from citizenship in a cultural sense and ignores their contributions. Because the ethnic Japanese are not only numerically but politically dominant, however, they are able to impose their ethnic primordiality as the official identity of the nation, ignoring divergent primordialities of ethnic minorities.

But no modern state can base its citizenship purely on ethnic primordial sentiments. The Japanese government is no exception. It has introduced civic sentiments calling forth more general, even 'universal' values, such as political freedom, democracy, civil rights, human dignity, and equality, which can presumably be shared by all groups. The problem is that these civic sentiments are only superficially overlaid on more deeply seated primordial sentiments spelled out in *Nihonjinron*.

This definition of the Japanese, based as it is on Japanese ethnic homogeneity, excludes Koreans and other minorities from the fold, precisely as Tamils, who are Hindus, are excluded from the Buddhist Sri Lankan cultural citizenship and Muslim Arabs living in Israel proper (not in the occupied territories) are excluded from being culturally part of the Israeli state, which is founded on Judaism. To be culturally Sri Lankan means to be a Sinhalese and a Buddhist, and to be culturally Israeli is to be a Jew and to espouse Judaism. In the same sense, according to the precepts of *Nihonjinron*, to be culturally Japanese means to be Japanese-Japanese, not Korean-Japanese or Ainu-Japanese. Where primordial and civic sentiments contradict each other, civic sentiments yield to the primordial ethnic definition of Japanese nationality. Koreans in Japan who insist on their civil rights are thus refused these rights because they are not ethnically Japanese.

The same dilemma of needing to accommodate ethnic minorities in other modern states that define themselves in terms of the dominant group seems to be the root problem in many if not most nation-states today. Is this not one of the issues for the Kurds and Armenians in Turkey, Algerians in France, Turkish *Gastarbeiters* in Germany, and Kurds in Iraq, as well as Arabs in Israel and Tamils in Sri Lanka?

National identity over the world is at a critical point, crying for revision and redefinition to bring ethnic minorities into the fold by adopting civic rather than primordial sentiments as a way of unifying the nation. Such a redefinition does not seek to eliminate primordiality of ethnic groups but to disaggregate it from the issue of national identity and leave the latter to civic sentiments capable of embracing heterogeneous ethnic groups. Unless such a course of action is taken, the ethnic strife we now see in all parts of the world will not only continue but will no doubt increase in the twenty-first century. It is in this light that we will explore political implications of cultural symbolism in relation to *Nihonjinron* in the next chapter.

# 5  Symbolic Vacuum

In the last several chapters we have examined specifics of *Nihonjinron* – its contents, its tenets, its players, its consumers, its ideological functions, and the like. In the next three chapters we turn to a larger issue of what *Nihonjinron* as a body of knowledge means to the Japanese. Having said this, I must immediately qualify the scope of this discussion. We have seen that tenets of *Nihonjinron* are not espoused by anything like all Japanese, but more like about half of them, according to the 1987 Nishinomiya survey (Befu and Manabe 1989, 1991). Thus our focus is on what *Nihonjinron* means to those who embrace its propositions. A discourse about half of the Japanese may not be about all Japanese, but it still is a discussion about a significant portion of the population.

Hundreds of books have been published on *Nihonjinron* in the postwar years to satisfy the voracious appetite of the Japanese seeking their national and cultural identity. Although there are many reasons for this boom, I would like to suggest one of them in this chapter, namely, that the use of previous symbols of national identity and pride was made problematic by World War II and that *Nihonjinron* moved into this relative identity vacuum.

## Instruments of National Identity

Cultural manifestations of nationalism come in a variety of forms: physical symbols, personages, rituals, and discourses. Every nation uses these instruments as a way of creating a sense of national identity, reminding its citizens of the importance of patriotism, and bolstering loyalty to the nation. The most obvious symbols of national identity are the national flag, the national anthem, the national emblem, and the national monuments and rituals, which are all physical representations of national identity and national pride. These symbols acquire an aura of sacredness and inviolability, and are designed to cause a surge of patriotic emotion when displayed at the right time in the proper place.

Every modern nation-state has these symbols and makes use of them to instill and reinforce sentiments of national unity and patriotism. They are a reminder of the importance of the state, which presumably protects its people but at the same time can ask them to sacrifice themselves for the sake of the state.

These symbols, it is important to note, are a creation of the state. Most of them did not emerge from the grass roots. Instead, they are consciously created by the state to promote national integration and to represent the state. Desecration of these symbols thus is an insult to the state, if not a crime.

Japan has had such symbols ever since it entered the modern period and began to have intercourse with Western nations. To be counted among the ranks of Western nations, Japan, too, had to acquire the proper accoutrements of a modern nation, including national symbols. And these symbols were widely used with nearly universal acceptance until the end of the World War II. With defeat, Japan was no longer able to exploit effectively the most important symbols expressing national identity and nationalism: the imperial institution, the 'national' flag, the 'national' anthem, the 'national' emblem, and national monuments and state rituals. The terms *flag* and *anthem* are modified with 'national' in quotation marks for reasons made clear in this chapter. The popularity of *Nihonjinron* in postwar Japan, I would argue, is a consequence of that inability.

## Imperial Institution

Royalty, if a nation has such an institution, is one of the most obvious and useful symbols of national identity. Most royal houses nowadays are stripped of real power, and are therefore less problematic as a symbolic source of national unity. No one can blame a powerless institution for real on imagined ills. Figurehead royalty can enjoy the prestige and honor inherent in the venerable institution. Witness Denmark, whose queen is a pride of the nation. Witness Great Britain, whose queen is also an undisputed national symbol. To be sure, some citizens are indifferent or antipathetic to the royalty in these countries. However, there is no deep-seated and widespread resentment toward or outright opposition to the institution. Not so in Japan.

The emperor and the imperial institution are perhaps the most outstanding symbols of modern Japan as a political entity. Before Japan launched its modernization program in 1868, the emperor occupied a relatively unimportant place in the minds of ordinary people. Many did not even know who the emperor was. One of the first tasks of the Meiji government was to 'modernize' the emperor and the imperial institution, which meant to make the emperor into a national symbol by 'Europeanizing' him (Fujitani 1996). The emperor was made to dress in Western clothing reminiscent of European royalty and was prominently displayed to the public on all major occasions of national celebration. He was displayed to the public in Western-style military uniform reviewing Japan's armed forces, for example. His uniformed figure was seen more and more frequently in the 1930s and 1940s as war efforts continued in frenzy until 1945. Because the emperor was the ultimate source of authority, all wars were fought under the imperial command and with his authorization.

This imperial involvement in past wars, especially World War II, made the Showa emperor Hirohito and the imperial institution itself into tainted and ambiguous symbols. Except for a small number of ultra-right-wing reactionaries, the Japanese now agree that war in general is bad and that the last war in particular was a horrendous mistake. Although they have not agreed on whom to blame and where to lay the responsibility for the war, many believe that the Showa emperor must at least share the blame.

This fact was dramatized at the death of the Showa emperor. Upon his death, the media questioned his role and responsibility for initiating, continuing, and terminating World War II. The Japanese government, under the conservative Liberal Democratic Party, along with other conservatives, took the position that the emperor was not responsible for initiating World War II. These groups maintained that the war was started by politicians and that the emperor as a constitutional monarch had no choice but to accept the political decision. The emperor himself took this position.

The establishment view, however, gives credit to the emperor for terminating the war. According to this view, the emperor had to intervene in this political decision because the factions for continuing the war and those favoring terminating it and surrendering were evenly split, thus forcing the emperor to make the decision; being benevolent, he made the right decision for the people. Some Japanese, however, feel that this reasoning is not logically consistent (Katō 1976). If the emperor had the authority to make a political decision to end the war, they argue, he must have had the authority to make a political decision to initiate or not initiate the war as well. Moreover, wartime records are clear that the emperor rejoiced over Japan's military victories, demonstrating his approval of the war effort.

Guidelines for elementary and secondary school education issued in 1982 require students to 'deepen their understanding, respect, and love toward the emperor.' This was the first time since 1945 that government guidelines set forth requirements regarding learning about the emperor; they were, however, balanced by the requirements that students be taught about popular sovereignty as well. In the 1989 guidelines, however, mention of popular sovereignty disappeared, while the requirement to learn about the emperor as the symbol of the Japanese nation remained. These guidelines were argued heatedly among teachers, school administrators, and scholars of education, many of whom do not necessarily see the meaning of the emperor in modern Japan in an entirely positive light.

The malaise that many Japanese felt toward the Showa emperor and the imperial institution he represented was poignantly expressed in the profound emotion expressed in the tragic experience of Okinawa. The emotion Okinawans feel when they think about the past war is well expressed in the following excerpts from an article that Arasaki Moriteru, president of Okinawa University, wrote in the January 10, 1989, issue of the *Mainichi Shimbun* soon after the death of Emperor Hirohito.[19]

> Japan is in mourning for the late Emperor Hirohito, but many Okinawans harbor mixed emotions about the monarch. In the second world war, Okinawa was the only major home island to experience ground fighting. Thousands of noncombatants committed suicide to avoid capture. In the bitter three-month battle 12,500 American and 110,000 Japanese military personnel, and 150,000 civilians were killed...

It was a shock to learn after the war that Hirohito could have prevented the invasion. In February 1945, with Allied Forces closing in, Prince Konoe Fumimaro, former prime minister and imperial confidant, urged Hirohito to end the war quickly. The monarch refused...The fateful decision turned the Ryukyus into a killing ground.

Shortly after World War II, Hirohito toured Japan...to emphasize that the people, not the emperor, were sovereign, a principle enshrined in the new [postwar] constitution. He did not go to Okinawa, however...Nor did he visit the prefecture in 1972 to welcome Okinawa back into the national fold. An Okinawan tour [by the emperor] required elaborate planning to ensure the emperor's safety...In 1975, the crown prince and princess tested the water and found it dangerous. The visit sparked violent protests, including a fire-bomb attack on the royal couple.

Another 12 years passed before Tokyo officials were ready to risk an imperial visit. In 1987, they announced that Hirohito, Crown Prince Akihito and his son, Prince Hiro, would attend the 42nd National Athletic Meet in Okinawa in October...When the emperor fell ill and was hospitalized in September 1987, Akihito, the crown prince, the crown princess and Prince Hiro went, anyway, over the protest by many Okinawans.

Okinawans see themselves exploited by the Japan to the north, or the Japanese government. First of all, Okinawa's sovereignty was stolen by the Meiji government, which forcibly annexed Okinawa to Japan. Second, Okinawa was made into a buffer between the rest of Japan and the Allied forces near the end of the war. Third, Okinawans see their territory as a sacrificial lamb offered by the emperor to the Allied forces to save the rest of Japan from prolonged occupation. Fourth and last, because most of the U.S. military installations are in Okinawa, the people see themselves as having been made into a buffer between the United States and the Communist bloc in the cold war and post–cold war era. Okinawans thus single themselves out as occupying a special and tragic place in contemporary Japanese history. Yet their suffering may be regarded as a heightened experience of what all Japanese experienced in the death of loved ones in war and in Allied bombings, in the postwar military occupation, and in being turned into a buffer between the United States and the Communist bloc.

Similarly, the public pronouncement by the mayor of Nagasaki (made in 1989, at a time the emperor was gravely ill), that Emperor Hirohito was responsible for the last war, echoed the opinion of many Japanese both in and north of Okinawa. To be sure, the mayor had license for the pronouncement because Nagasaki, having been one of two cities in Japan – and in the world – to be atom-bombed. Like Okinawa, Nagasaki and Hiroshima suffered more intensively what all other Japanese experienced – in these cities' case because of the atom bomb and its aftermath. Bitterness runs close to the surface there, and when (in 1989, at a time when the emperor was gravely ill) the mayor of Nagasaki publicly declared that Emperor Hirohito was responsible for the last war, he echoed the opinion of many Japanese both in and north of Okinawa. The pronouncement rang true for many Japanese elsewhere who would have been reluctant to say such things outright.

The issue of the last emperor's responsibility in World War II had been brewing under the surface until his death on January 7, 1989. That the issue surfaced and was much debated in the media immediately upon his death indicated the extent to which the Japanese public had held an equivocal position with regard to the emperor's role in the war. The Japan Communist Party predictably boycotted his funeral on February 24. Socialists attended, but only after objecting to the lack of clear separation of state and religion in the funeral. Many groups held meetings throughout the country to voice their objections to the use of state funds for the funeral and to discuss the emperor's role in the last war.

These considerations make it clear that the imperial institution in Japan is not a clear and unequivocal symbol of national unity. Rather, it contains a dangerously divisive element. Thus we cannot equate the role of the imperial institution in Japan with the role of royalty in England, Norway, or Denmark. Norwegians remember their king as having threatened to abdicate if the country surrendered to the Nazis. Hirohito did not suggest a similar threat to the military when it deliberated the possibility of starting the Pacific war.

The 'mistake' of the last emperor in leading the Japanese people into war is deeply felt by many Japanese, and this feeling is in part expressed in the extent to which they have overwhelmingly defended the 'Peace Constitution,' whose Article 9 renounces war. Ultra-conservatives would like to see a constitutional revision that would allow Japan to take up arms legitimately, but a great majority of Japanese oppose such a revision. Their opposition shows the depth of antiwar feelings the Japanese have. Many, though not all, link their conviction directly to the role of the emperor in the last war.

## The 'National' Flag

If the imperial institution is in jeopardy as a symbol of national identity and unity, so are the 'Japanese' flag, the 'national' anthem, and the national emblem. In understanding the controversy over the flag and the anthem of Japan, it is well to remember that their legal status was in limbo until 1999 when a special law was passed to define them as *national*. Until then, nothing in the current constitution or the postwar statute book specified and defined the official flag or the official song of the Japanese state. It was only by convention carried over from the prewar era that the flag with a round red center and white background – commonly called *Hinomaru* – was regarded as the 'national' flag and the song that begins '*Kimigayo wa*,' the 'national' anthem. This absence of statutory specification gave critics of the use of *Hinomaru* and *Kimigayo* ammunition to fight their uses as official national symbols. Critics would not refer to *Hinomaru* as *kokki* (the national flag) or *Kimigayo* as *kokka* (the national anthem).

Before August 16, 1945, every Japanese house was required to display the *Hinomaru* flag on every occasion of national celebration. Moreover, the flag was an integral part of the war effort. Whenever Japan won a war, as with the Sino-Japanese War of 1894–95 and the Russo-Japanese War of 1904–05, the flag was displayed all over Japan to celebrate the country's victory. During the Sino-Japanese 'conflict' that started in 1937, too, the flag was an indispensable symbol for celebrating Japan's military victories, such as the fall of Nanking or the takeover of Shanghai. Flags were displayed in front of houses, and participants in victory marches each waved a small handheld flag.

Too, the flag was indispensable for seeing new military recruits off to barracks. On the day a recruit was to leave home, neighbors gathered in front of his house, where the flag was displayed. After the recruit, the head of the neighborhood association, and other public officials made speeches, everyone shouted 'banzai' for the send-off and waved handheld flags.

After World War II, display of the 'national' flag was restricted, though not totally banned, by the Occupation precisely because it was implicated in Japan's war efforts. Even after the Occupation Forces left, however, displaying the flag was such an anathema that for many years the flag was seldom shown even on major national holidays (Anzu 1972). Even now many Japanese hesitate to display it in front of their homes for fear of being misidentified as ultra–right-wing conservatives. Businesses, too, shy away from using the national flag. The appropriateness of displaying the flag is still widely debated in the media because flag use has become associated with reactionary politics and right-wing hooliganism.

A 1989 manual issued by the Ministry of Education specifies that the flag be raised and the Kimigayo anthem sung at the ceremony for entering students and at graduation; on other occasions, use of these symbols was left up to the discretion of school administrators. That the ministry had to issue a directive urging the use of the 'national' flag and 'national' anthem is a comment on the controversial nature of their use in Japan. It indicated that not all schools had been displaying the flag on these occasions and that school officials did not agree on displaying the *Hinomaru* flag and singing the *Kimigayo* anthem.

During the stormy anti–security treaty demonstrations of 1960 and the equally turbulent anti-establishment movement of the late 1960s, demonstrators used anything but the national flag as the symbol of their cause. Until the 1990s, when the annual 'Spring Offensive' labor demonstration took place, oversized red banners dominated the scene. Thus it is not a surprise that a Korean youth asked Chung In-Wha (1987), a reporter writing for *Shokun*, 'Why do Japanese demonstrators carry red flags but not the national flag?'

The flag, as a symbol of war, is implicated in all the sufferings Okinawans had to endure toward the end of the war, as well as after the war under the long period of occupation by Allied Powers, lasting far beyond the occupation of the rest of Japan. One flag-burning incident in Yomitan underscores the anathematic nature of the flag (Shimojima 1988). Near the end of World War II, the

Japanese army built an air strip in the village of Yomitan, where the incident took place. When the Allied forces began landing on Okinawa, this village was not spared. Villagers, 139 in number, fled to a nearby valley known as Chibirigama, and in the end, 82 of them killed themselves or killed one another to escape capture by the enemy. It is a story so painful and gruesome to recall that everyone in the village wanted to obliterate it from memory, and they had, until the incidence was unearthed by a writer from north of Okinawa (Shimojima 1984). The villagers blamed the wartime Japanese authority – including the emperor – for this tragedy. To add further pain, after the war American Occupation Forces moved into the village and established military facilities whose removal became the prime political issue for the village. After their removal, an athletic field was constructed on the site.

In December 1986, the village assembly of Yomitan passed a resolution opposing the government's attempt to force people to accept *Hinomaru* and *Kimigayo*. When Yomitan was selected as the site of the softball game for the National Athletic Meet in 1987, which occasioned visitation by the Crown Prince and his entourage, the village assembly voted, not surprisingly, not to sing the *Kimigayo* anthem and not to raise the *Hinomaru* flag for the occasion. But only four days before the event, the Softball Association president threatened to move the game to another site if the village did not agree to raise the Hinomaru flag. This was an attempt to take advantage of a sporting event for political coercion: the village was forced to rescind its decision. When the flag was hoisted, however, an angry villager took it down and burned it.

The wartime and postwar experiences of Okinawans, including those of Yomitan village, are well expressed in their treatment of the Japanese flag. According to a 1985 government survey, only 6 percent of middle schools and none of the of high schools in Okinawa raised the Hinomaru flag at commencement (Noda 1988: 158). Consequently, the Prefectural Department of Education, representing the central government, issued 'administrative guidance' that read in part, 'We ask you to provide strong guidance for students' deepened understanding of the educational significance of the national flag and the national anthem and to take positive steps to raise the national flag and sing the national anthem at school events' (Anonymous 1984). After much pressure, including sanctions against those not following the guidance, 70 percent of the schools in Okinawa, including Yomitan High School, raised the flag at commencement in 1986. In the following year, however, one female student dragged down the flag during the commencement in protest against the symbol of aggression that began the Second World War.

In 1988, the flag issue continued to plague schools in Okinawa. At Urazoe Industrial High School, only about half the graduating seniors rose to their feet when the flag was raised. At Nakanishi Middle School, graduating seniors boycotted the commencement because the flag was being displayed. They refused to enter the assembly hall and demanded that school officials take the flag down, although in the end, students acceded and attended the ceremony.

In short, in the absence of national consensus on the use of national symbols – whether the emperor, the national flag, or the national anthem – the government is imposing nationalism upon students, forcing school officials to demonstrate nationalism even though some may not be prepared to do so.

## The 'National' Anthem

If *Hinomaru* is problematic as a postwar symbol of Japan, *Kimigayo* is even more so because it is integrally tied in with another problematic symbol, namely the imperial institution. The verse in *Kimigayo* celebrates the eternal prosperity of the imperial line. In 1989 the Ministry of Education issued an instructor's manual that specified that the term *kimi* – which has several dictionary meanings, including 'you' – specifically designated the emperor here. Ten years later, when the government introduced a bill to legislate *Kimigayo* as the national anthem, the government took the same position. According to ministerial guidelines, the national anthem is a song that expresses the wish that our nation will prosper. Here, 'our nation' and the emperor are treated synonymously. Speaking for the passage of the national flag/national anthem bill, in 1999 Prime minister Obuchi took the stand that *Kimigayo* as the national anthem and *Hinomaru* as the national flag represented the 'collective will of the people (*kokumin no sōi*).' Given the strong and deep-seated opposition among ordinary Japanese, 'collective will' seemed to be Obuchi's wishful thinking. Writing in the U.S.

satellite edition *Asahi Shinbun* (June 8, 1989), Professor Yamazumi Masaki of Tokyo Metropolitan University, a critic of mandated use of *Hinomaru* and *Kimigayo*, argued that students should be taught how these symbols were exploited before and during the last war before being required to respect them.

Given this background, it is not surprising that *Kimigayo* is not welcomed by many Japanese. Even after the 'administrative guidance' requiring students and teachers to show respect to the national anthem, half the graduating seniors at Urazoe Industrial High School remained seated, instead of standing as expected, when a tape of the song was broadcast at commencement in 1988. According to a survey by the Okinawa Prefectural Department of Education, only at 3.4 percent of elementary schools and 7.8 percent of middle schools was *Kimigayo* sung at graduation in 1988. Only two high schools adopted *Kimigayo* at graduation, and only a taped recording was broadcast rather than having the students sing it. In noticeable contrast, 100 percent of the elementary schools raised the flag at graduation in the same year. What explains the big difference between use of the flag and use of the anthem?

One reason is that singing requires active participation by students, whereas one need only passively observe a flag being raised. It is easier to be a bystander of nationalism rather than being an active participant of it. Another reason is that the narrative meaning of the flag – what the red and white colors signify – is muted and only implied rather than being explicit. In contrast, *Kimigayo* clearly narrates the centrality of the emperor in the Japanese nation. Understandably, resistance to active singing is stronger than passive observation.

The resistance to singing *Kimigayo* on the part of schoolteachers and students and the pressure to force its adoption by the government are an irresistible force meeting an immovable power. Tragic is the person caught between them, like Mr. Toshihiro Ishikawa, a high school principal in Hiroshima Prefecture. On February 28, 1999, Mr. Ishikawa hanged himself on the eve of the graduation day, when singing of *Kimigayo* was mandated. He had been caught between the Prefectural Board of Education, representing the Ministry of Education of the central government, which had been pressuring him to display the *Hinomaru* flag and sing the *Kimigayo* anthem at the graduation, on one hand, and members of teachers' unions opposing the government position. Principal Ishikawa spent months working with both sides without being able to resolve the difference. His final solution was to take his own life.

Immediately after this incident, the government swiftly moved to introduce a bill to make *Kimigayo* the national anthem and *Hinomaru* the national flag. Opposition political parties proposed to take time and have thorough deliberation involving ordinary citizens, which was in part a stalling tactic. But those in power were anxious for quick results. Afraid of the bill's not reaching the floor during the current parliamentary session and thus being killed, the government managed to extend the session. The bill was introduced on June 11, and on August 9 it became law.[20]

Passage of a bill, however, does not establish national consensus, nor does it prove presence of 'a collective will' of the people. What it does is harden the government position, giving it legal authority – not to say legitimacy – to coerce people and institutions to use the national flag and anthem. Legislation of the bill did not change the attitude of most people, though some no doubt would consider legislation a good enough reason to follow government guidelines. But legislation also has the opposite effect of widening the gap between the government position now buttressed by law and the attitude of those who oppose the use of reminders of Japan's tarnished war.

## National Monuments

National monuments, such as the tomb of an unknown soldier, serve to create and reinforce patriotism. Although Japan does have such a tomb, it, like the soldiers entombed therein, is virtually unknown to the public. Much better known – in fact universally known in Japan – is the Yasukuni Shrine in Tokyo, which enshrines the souls of all soldiers who died for the country in wars since the time of the Meiji restoration. Until the end of World War II, Yasukuni played a pivotal role in bolstering patriotism. It is of critical importance for us that the only significant criterion for being enshrined at Yasukuni is that one 'has died in war for the emperor.' Nearly two and a half million souls are enshrined there (Ōe 1984). Yasukuni was easily integrated into the state Shinto theology, where the war dead became Shinto gods and spiritual protectors of the nation. Nationalism and militaristic jingoism thus became one in Yasukuni. Whereas the tombs of unknown soldiers in Western countries are not explicitly religious, the Shinto character of Yasukuni gives it a ready aura of sacredness. This religious basis made it convenient to drum up patriotism, since patriotism – and nationalism, for that matter – is a form of civil religion (Hiro and Yamamoto 1986), an idea we shall take up in the following chapter.

Until the end of the war, Yasukuni and most other major Shinto shrines were supported by the state. After World War II, as a result of the constitutional separation of the state and religion, Yasukuni became a private religious corporation (National Diet Library, Research and Legislative Reference Department 1976). Despite this constitutional requirement for total separation, the conservative government wishes to use Yasukuni for its political goals, as was done before and during World War II (Etō and Kobori 1986; Kogawa 1988).

This shrine is problematic and controversial as a symbol of national unity, however, precisely because it memorializes and commemorates – even celebrates – not only those who were drafted into the imperial army against their will but also the war criminals such as Tōjō Hideki who were tried in the Tokyo war tribunal and hanged for their 'crimes against humanity.' In fact, it is so problematic that there is an ongoing public debate whether the prime minister and his cabinet members should visit Yasukuni Shrine, especially on August 15, the anniversary of the end of the Pacific war (Kamiya 1987).

Objections to government officials' visits to Yasukuni have been raised from many sectors of the society and in many forms, including lawsuits brought by citizens groups. But in particular they came from a most unexpected corner. On August 15, 1988, more than a hundred relatives of the war dead who are enshrined at Yasukuni, organized by the National Alliance of Relatives of War Dead for Peace (Heiwa Izoku-kai Zenkoku Renraku-kai), marched in Tokyo with the slogan, 'Don't glorify war. Stop [cabinet ministers'] official visits to Yasukuni Shrine.' According to the media, even right-wing ultra-nationalists, widely known for riding around in vans blaring the national anthem and wartime patriotic songs, were respectful of the marchers.

In addition to the constitutional and other objections raised by Japanese citizens, visits of government officials to Yasukuni are also opposed by Japan's neighbors, who were victims of the last war. They, particularly China, see government officials' visits to Yasukuni as Japan's attempt to legitimize the illegitimate war and everything done in the name of the war by the Japanese military, such as the Nanking massacre. It is noteworthy that because of the shrine's problematic nature, no foreign head of state has ever visited Yasukuni. This non-practice starkly contrasts with the virtually mandatory visit of foreign heads of state to the tombs of unknown soldiers in other countries.

Thus three issues overlie one another with respect to the Yasukuni Shrine: (1) popular disdain for Yasukuni as a symbol of the patriotism that led Japan to disaster and for using the shrine to legitimate an illegitimate war; (2) the constitutional separation of religion and the state, which high government officials flout by visiting the shrine; and (3) delicate international politics, where Japan's Asian neighbors – who suffered from Japan's militarism – watch worriedly for any sign of militaristic resurgence in Japan (Futaba and Umehara 1976).

## Public Rituals

Public rituals are an effective means of fostering and bolstering nationalism and national identity. Every nation takes advantage of seasonal or cyclical rituals for this purpose. National rituals are important for calling forth a sense of belonging to a nation and oneness with the state. The coronation of a king or a queen is an obvious example of an occasion when a whole nation is expected to participate in the celebration of the national rite of passage (Cannadine 1983). In the United States, the presidential inauguration, which takes place every four years, rivals a coronation. Anzac Day in Australia (Kapferer 1988) and Remembrance Day and Independence Day in Israel (Handelman, 1990) are also examples of rituals of national and patriotic import.

We saw earlier that school commencement is being used by the Japanese government to promote patriotism, loyalty, and nationalism through forced adoption of the *Hinomaru* flag and the *Kimigayo* anthem. We also saw that as long as such rituals are associated with the imperial institution and the ill-fated World War II, they create problems: they are divisive and provoke anxiety. An even better example is the funeral of the last emperor.

Citizens groups also raised objections to the ceremony for the enthronement of the new emperor, Akihito. The National Conference to Guard against Erosion of Separation of the State and Religion (Seikyō Bunri no Shingai o Kanshi suru Zenkoku Kaigi) passed a resolution objecting to the enthronement and presented a petition against it to the Diet. Although the issue in theory is the constitutional separation of the state and religion, as a practical agenda, these groups were attempting to limit the role of the imperial institution in fostering nationalistic and patriotic spirit in Japan, and thus in defining Japan's identity.

## Symbolic Vacuum

All these cases, whether the Showa emperor's funeral, Emperor Akihito's coronation, or government officials' visits to Yasukuni, point to the equivocal and controversial nature of major national symbols and rituals for integrating the nation and defining the national identity.

This brings us back to the symbolic vacuum hypothesis I alluded to at the beginning of this chapter. It seems to me that *Nihonjinron* has moved in to occupy the identity space vacated by tainted symbols of dubious credibility. A caveat is in order. *Nihonjinron*, as a discourse, lacks the strong emotional content that the national flag and other physical and institutional symbols have and so is not a complete, functional substitute. Nonetheless, it is useful to examine the relationship between the discourse of national identity and the national symbols, which forms a continuum in terms of amount of narrative content on one hand and emotional content on the other. These two variables are, generally speaking, negatively correlated.

At one end are symbols with a minimum of descriptive or discursive contents, such as the flag; at the other is *Nihonjinron* literature, which defines in discourse the national and cultural identity. Somewhere in the middle are national symbols with some discursive elements, such as the national anthem, which in a few terse lines tries to inform singers and listeners of the distilled essence of the national identity. Rituals, though usually lacking in extensive narrative content, provide some descriptive meaning in the speeches that usually accompany them. *Nihonjinron* is strong precisely where symbols are weak: namely, it explicitly defines national identity and explains why one should be proud of one's nation.

Insofar as emotional commitment and hortative contents are concerned, physical symbols, monuments, and rituals are strong as discourses are weak. They conjure up emotional identification with the nation and motivate citizens to be patriotic without words or with few words. Some discourses of nationalism, such as Hitler's *Mein Kampf*, or Mao's 'little red book' can bring out emotion; but most discourses lack the powerful and immediate emotional force that symbolic forms of nationalism have.

In the absence of major national symbols of identity that can unequivocally unify the Japanese nation, *Nihonjinron* as a discourse of cultural nationalism can substitute to the extent that these symbols have discursive contents, both descriptive and hortative, and to the extent that *Nihonjinron* can arouse readers emotionally as physical symbols do. It is, at least in part, in the relative symbolic vacuum, I would argue, that *Nihonjinron* has entered the arena of postwar nationalism as a way of defining Japan's new identity, unblemished by past symbols. The convenience of *Nihonjinron* as a discourse is that its contents can be readily altered: the *Nihonjinron* of the war years is not the same as that of the postwar era. Flexibility of discourse allows different contents to be emphasized according to the needs of the age.

As we shall see in Chapter Seven, contents of *Nihonjinron* have altered radically from time to time. In fact, the discussion has turned 180 degrees since World War II. The wartime *Nihonjinron* was dominated by a state-sponsored, emperor-centered ideology. Postwar *Nihonjinron* entirely discarded the imperial institution and other problematic symbols of national identity associated with the military Japan of the past, while amplifying other aspects of pre-1945 *Nihonjinron* that were relatively minor when the imperial institution was the key element.

This sort of flexibility is not as easy to achieve in physical symbols. No doubt symbols need to be interpreted and they can be given new meanings. However, the interpretation of a flag or a monument cannot vary a great deal; it must remain within fairly narrowly prescribed parameters as defined by historical practices. The mental association of specific physical symbols with past events indelibly remains.

The substitution of a revised *Nihonjinron* for nationalistic symbols allows continuity of nationalistic ideology while rejecting the ideology directly associated with the past war. Both wartime *Nihonjinron* and postwar neo-*Nihonjinron* rely heavily on Japan's primordial sentiments inherent in the presumed 'ethnic essence' of the Japanese – blood, purity of race, language mystique, and so on. For example, the idea that the Japanese people are homogeneous and the Japanese culture is pure and unique, which formed the basis of the wartime nationalistic ideology, is repeated in postwar *Nihonjinron*. The familistic basis of the society, argued by Murakami, Kumon, and Satō (1979) in their postwar neo-*Nihonjinron*, mirrors the familistic argument propounded by wartime ideologues, placing the emperor as the father figure of a nation conceived of as a family writ large (Kawashima 1950, 1957). The notion that Japanese spiritualism can conquer Western materialism, propagandized during the last war to cover up the paucity of war matériel, is very much alive now. The notion that Japan is the best nation in the world, now prominently argued by ideologues of *Nihonjinron*, was, of course, part and parcel of the wartime *Nihonjinron*. What contemporary *Nihonjinron* does is to strip wartime *Nihonjinron* of its imperial and militaristic elements and re-dress it in a language devoid of war and militarism.

I am not arguing that this 'symbolic vacuum' hypothesis is a complete and adequate explanation for the postwar popularity of *Nihonjinron*; in other chapters I discuss other reasons for *Nihonjinron*'s popularity. Nor am I arguing that *Nihonjinron* entirely or adequately replaces symbols of nationalism in Japan, which are in jeopardy now.

Japan is groping for more adequate unifying symbols. Since much of the troubled situation of the imperial institution arises out of the role that the Showa emperor played in the Sino-Japanese War and the Pacific war, with his death and the enthronement of his son, Akihito who is not implicated in these events, the imperial institution now has a chance to restore its credibility to the Japanese people. The new emperor is much more 'democratic' in approach – addressing the Japanese people informally as *minasan* ('everyone' or 'you all'), instead of the more formal terms his father was wont to use, such as *shokun, nanji,* or *shinmin* ('ye subjects'). His marriage to a commoner also signaled a departure from his predecessors and the start of a new era. Thus the imperial institution may regain some role as a unifying symbol.

In thinking about the uses of *Hinomaru* as the national flag and *Kimigayo* as the national anthem we need to recognize the almost total absence of alternative symbols in the opposing discourse. Those opposing the legislation merely argued for 'thorough deliberation' to gain time, hopefully to allow the bill to expire, and also to have time to expose the shameful wartime implications of these symbols and thereby again oppositional momentum. But what no one and no party did was to propose an alternative design of a national flag and an alternative national anthem that could gain broad acceptance. Left without alternatives, the public and opposition parties could only oppose the government initiative without a replacement to be considered and to rally around. Opposition became a futile exercise only for the sake of opposing.

This situation is precisely repeated with respect to *Nihonjinron.* It is often asked why *Nihonjinron* maintains such a strong hold in Japanese society, when only about half of the population at best seem to support its tenets and propositions. I submit that it is the absence of any alternative worldview, cultural model, or ideology that people might consider and propose in place of *Nihonjinron* that allows this outmoded worldview to persist in spite of the wide and even widening gap between the reality of the Japanese society and the imagery supported in *Nihonjinron.* The Marxist model was suppressed by the government before 1945, to be sure, but after the war, even without government suppression, it never gained popularity. The stratification model (Mouer and Sugimoto 1986; Seiyama et al. eds. 2000), the conflict model (Krauss, Rohlen, and Steinhoff eds. 1984; Eisenstadt and Ben-Ari 1990), and the social exchange model (Itō 1995; Kuji 1988) of Japanese society are all purely academic – they remain in the ivory tower without gaining popularity among the general public. Without anyone being able to propose an alternative model that can gain widespread popular support, *Nihonjinron* will continue to have its day as the essentialized representation of Japan. It will play the hegemonic role as the dominant ideology of Japan. This role of *Nihonjinron* is manifested as the civil religion of Japan, as argued in the next chapter.

# 6  Civil Religion

We shall explore in this chapter the meaning of *Nihonjinron* by asking an uncommon question: Does *Nihonjinron* qualify as a religion? If so, in what sense is it a religion? Does it provide religious meaning to its believers, and if so how? We have two starting points. One is the idea of *Nihonkyō* (religion of Japan) proposed by Isiah BenDasan, to which he says all Japanese subscribe, whether they are Buddhists, Shintoists, Christians, or even the rare Muslims, as long they claim to be Japanese. BenDasan never once refers to *Nihonjinron*, but the basic tenets of his *Nihonkyō* come infinitely close to the propositions and assumptions of *Nihonjinron*.

The other starting point is the concept of civil religion. Robert Bellah and Winston Davis have already contributed to the concept of *Nihonjinron* as civil religion. This chapter will review their contributions, further extend the application of the concept, and integrate it with BenDasan's concept of *Nihonkyō*.

## BenDasan's Background

Among the postwar *Nihonjinron* books, we have noted Isaiah BenDasan's *Nihonjin to Yudayajin* (1970) as one of the runaway best-sellers, winning the coveted Ōya Sōichi nonfiction prize.[21] In an interview in 1984 (Usui 1984), Yamamoto Shichihei, who is now presumed by all to be the real Isaiah BenDasan, acknowledged sales of eight hundred thousand copies of the hardcover edition of the book and two million copies of the softcover. By 1989, the hardcover edition alone had been reprinted fifty times.

Its fresh approach – of comparing Japanese, not with Europeans, with whom the Japanese had been compared so often in the *Nihonjinron* literature, but with Jews – was a great appeal to the reader. Its easy, almost casual writing style was also a definite plus. Yet BenDasan's seeming erudition on Judaism, a religion totally foreign and exotic to most Japanese, as well as on Christianity, especially the Old Testament, was a factor rendering authenticity to the work.

BenDasan was a totally unknown quantity in the intellectual community until his book was published and became an instant hit. He apparently had no college degree and no academic position and had written no book except the one at issue, which was published by Yamamoto Shoten, owned by Yamamoto Shichihei himself. Yamamoto chose this approach most likely because without credentials and publishing records, he could not convince any publisher to accept his manuscript. The book was presented as an original Japanese work rather than a translation, in contrast to later BenDasan books. For example, *Nihonkyō ni tsuite* (On *Nihonkyō*) (1975), which was originally serialized in a magazine and later published in book form in hardcover and then in a paperback edition, was said to have been authored by BenDasan in a foreign language and translated by Yamamoto Shichihei into Japanese. In the following year BenDasan published another book on *Nihonkyō* (BenDasan 1976), which was again said to have been translated by Yamamoto Shichihei. A few years later, Yamamoto engaged Komuro Naoki in a dialogue in *Nihonkyō no shakaigaku* (The Sociology of *Nihonkyō*) (Yamamoto and Komuro 1981), the two together providing further elaboration on this subject. These works constitute the major sources of *Nihonkyō* discussed in this chapter.[22]

## *Nihonkyō*

In these sources, BenDasan offers a view that all Japanese, regardless of their official religious affiliation, belong to what he calls *Nihonkyō*, a religion to which all Japanese subscribe by sheer dint of being Japanese. According to BenDasan, being a Christian or a Buddhist in Japan simply means the person is of the Christian sect or the Buddhist sect of *Nihonkyō* (*Nihonkyōto Kirisuto-ha* or *Nihonkyōto Bukkyō-ha*). Other sects of *Nihonkyō* include the *Sōka Gakkai* sect and the *Marxist* sect (BenDasan 1970: 90).

It is a crazy idea, according to BenDasan, to think that one can change the faith of *Nihonkyō* believers to another religion, an idea that only Christian missionaries entertain seriously. As soon as a foreign religion like Christianity invades Japan, it simply transforms into a variety of *Nihonkyō*, a point that reminds one of Endō Shūsaku's *Silence* (1979). In fact, BenDasan has good company in Carlos Caldarola, who persuasively argues for the Japanization of Christianity (1979).

Komuro Naoki, who appears to be in complete agreement with Yamamoto – and BenDasan, too, naturally – with regard to the concept of *Nihonkyō*, captures the core of this religion when he says, 'It is no exaggeration to say that to understand *Nihonkyō* is to understand Japan and to understand the Japanese' (Yamamoto and Komuro 1981: 124). BenDasan claims that the Japanese are simply unaware of their affiliation to *Nihonkyō* and are blissfully living within the framework of *Nihonkyō*'s religious prescriptions and taboos without realizing the fact (1970: 90).

Turning now to more specific tenets of *Nihonkyō*, Yamamoto refers to the concept of 'air (*kūki*)' as a dogma. Any religion landing on the shore of Japan becomes spineless because *Nihonkyō*, by using its 'thorough-going 'principle of principle-lessness,'' makes the fundamental meaning of the intruding religion meaningless. This principle is what Yamamoto calls 'air,' further elaborated in a separate book on this subject (1983). The term *kūki* is used somewhat in the sense of implicit normative constraints. It is used as an explanation for doing or thinking whatever Japanese do or think. It becomes an excuse for what Japanese have done or have not done. Thus a Japanese would say, 'Because of the '*air*' of the time (or place), I had to (couldn't) do it.' And this would be regarded as a sufficient and legitimate reason without explaining further, in other words, without explaining the specific cultural assumptions that made the action legitimate (Yamamoto and Komuro 1981: 136). When a Japanese speaks, he does not just speak plain truth but filters this truth through this 'air.' Truth (*jijitsu*) then becomes culturally filtered truth, or *jitsujō*, which is another fundamental element of *Nihonkyō*. *Jitsujō* is truth or fact as altered or interpreted by human feelings and human relations.

To understand *Nihonkyō*, BenDasan recommends analyzing martyrs of *Nihonkyō*, many of whom are, by the way, featured in various books on 'the heart' of Japan discussed in earlier chapters. A prime example of these martyrs is Saigō Takamori, who according to BenDasan, is not only *Nihonkyō*'s martyr but also its saint. BenDasan claims Saigō's writings are those of a great religious person and not of a politician. According to BenDasan, Saigō viewed humans as part of 'nature,' which is governed by a principle called 'the way (*michi*),' which is best understood as 'the Japanese philosophy of life' or as 'the Japanese principle of the universe.' Humans are to practice this principle, and Saigō is supposed to be a paragon of this moral virtue.

The importance of *michi* in *Nihonjinron* is obvious. It is the fundamental concept underlying all Japanese traditional arts and crafts. Though the term *michi* may not be explicitly used in nontraditional fields of learning, the concept behind it is very much adopted, even in corporate settings, school sports, and other activities. The Chinese character for *michi* is the same as that for *dō*, as in jūdō, aikidō, and *sadō* (the way of the tea ceremony). The term points to the common philosophical foundation of all traditional arts in Japan, which are emphasized in *Nihonjinron*, thus linking *Nihonkyō* to *Nihonjinron*.

BenDasan also emphasizes the importance of the Japanese language in *Nihonkyō*, he calls it the 'religious language' of *Nihonkyō*, as Latin was once the religious language of the Catholic Church. Roy Andrew Miller (1982) has engaged in extensive discussion of the mythical qualities that the Japanese claim for their language. Unaware of the concept of *Nihonkyō*, Miller does not quite consider Japanese as the religious language of the Japanese, but his contentions about the Japanese view of the language would support BenDasan's argument. The fundamental assumption is that the language itself provides religious teaching (BenDasan 1975: 22). This is seen when Japanese argue and try to make a point. They do not present a logical demonstration; instead they try to persuade others through feeling and emotion (BenDasan 1975: 21). And the persuasiveness of the argument is predicated on the affective use of Japanese – that is, the use of its in-built facility for conveying emotions – and the understanding of the premises of *Nihonkyō*.

Those who write about the 'logic' of Japanese thought processes or the 'logic' of the Japanese language argue that the Japanese reasoning process is not merely a matter of Aristotelian logic, but is imbued with feelings and particularistic considerations. This we have seen in earlier chapters, and is in essence what BenDasan argues here:

Among Japanese, there is the concept of *ningen* (human), from which emanate what the Japanese consider fundamental and universal tenets. They try to persuade each other on the basis of these tenets; they do not try to construct a logical argument. The tenets are subconscious, but are so firmly believed in and upheld that they do not even harbor the possibility that you may not believe in them (BenDasan 1975: 22).

An understanding of the language, not only in its linguistic aspects but in its extralinguistic aspects as well, is the sine qua non for the appreciation of *Nihonkyō*, as well as of *Nihonjinron*. Yet, BenDasan admits, this is a feat impossible for foreigners, including himself (BenDasan 1970: 94–95) – though as Yamamoto Shichihei, I am sure he would have no problem at all.

*Nihonkyō* requires understanding, first, of the extralinguistic language of Japanese, that is, that which is only implicit in verbalized statements, and, second, of 'the extra-legal law' of Japan, that is, customary prescriptions that are only implied and not explicitly stated in law (BenDasan 1970: 95). What he calls 'humanology (*ningengaku*)' is discussed in this extralinguistic language and in extralegal prescriptions. This makes it extremely difficult for foreigners to achieve full comprehension of the humanological 'theology' of *Nihonkyō* (BenDasan 1970: 104). To understand this extralegal law means to appreciate the fact that in the court of law, whether one is a judge, a plaintiff, or a defendant, one has to be first and last a *Nihonkyō* faithful. One is first and last judged on the basis of how 'pure (*junsui*),' or good a Japanese one is.

If *Nihonkyō* is a religion, does it have sacraments? Of course, one would not find rituals corresponding to Catholic sacraments, but there are functional equivalents in *Nihonkyō*, according to Yamamoto and Komuro (1981: 158–218), though the use of the term 'sacrament' in this context is dubious. They list seven cardinal sacramental concepts: 'nature (*shizen*),' 'true intention (*honshin*),' 'facts (*jitsujō*),' 'person (*ningen*),' 'purity (*junsui*),' 'order (*joretsu*),' and 'marriage (*kekkon*).' These concepts are closely interrelated. Often they are defined in terms of one another and imply each other. They are, as we shall see, familiar ingredients of Nihonjinron and what Winston Davis calls 'value-traces' of civil religion (Davis 1973: 2), the fundamental values and assumptions of Japanese culture by which the Japanese order their lives.

BenDasan conceptualizes 'nature (*shizen*)' as inner psychic order, social order, and natural order, all three packed in one. *Nihonjinron* expresses this same idea in terms of harmony with nature, harmony in the social order, and inner tranquility, emphasizing interdependence of the three types of harmony.

'Intention (*honshin*)' is the essence of sincerity, emanating from purity of heart. It is best exemplified in a newborn baby, who is full of 'good' (*zen*) and behaves according to the order of the universe and the principle of nature.

Rather than naked fact, 'fact (*jitsujō*)' in *Nihonkyō* is fact enveloped in human and particularistic considerations. Decisions are to be made on the basis of human feelings and human relationships as much as on the basis of factual information.

Another of the fundamental tenets of *Nihonkyō* is its human-centeredness. *Nihonkyō* is not about heaven or gods, it is about how humans relate to one another. BenDasan quotes a passage from Natsume Sōseki's *Kusamakura*: 'The world where we live was made by neither gods nor demons...It consists of your honest neighbors who are busily getting about on your right, your left and opposite' (Natsume 1927: 1–2).

BenDasan devised a clever expression, 'your you (*omae no omae*).' Or, 'I exist only as your 'other'.' That is, reference to oneself has no meaning in Japanese society except as a person in relationship with another. Self thus is defined from the point of view of the other, the person with whom the '*watashi*' is interacting. In *Nihonkyō* there is no theology, only humanology, according to BenDasan (1970: 104).

The crucial importance of interpersonal relationships in Japanese society is argued by Hamaguchi (1977), Nakane (1967), and many others of *Nihonjinron* persuasion. They each differ in many details, important as they are for individual theorists; nonetheless they, including BenDasan, point to the self-same fundamentality of human relationships in Japan.

'Purity (*junsui*)' is an idea already touched on in connection with 'intention (*honshin*).' All persons, that is to say, all Japanese, are said to have 'pure heart.' In *Nihonkyō*, one can claim clear conscience as long as one's action is based on 'purity of heart.'

'Order (*joretsu*)' has to do with vertical social order, which has been made well known to us through Nakane's work, although BenDasan makes no reference to Nakane. A hierarchical social order is a fundamental principle of human organization in *Nihonjinron*, and observance of this order is absolutely essential for *Nihonkyō* followers.

Thus, although BenDasan's ideas are clothed in his own idiosyncratic language, they parallel or dovetail ideas expressed in the language of *Nihonjinron*. The only difference – a critical difference – is that he has named this domain of thought *Nihonkyō* and recognized it as the religion of the Japanese. Moreover, he has argued that it transcends normal religions like Buddhism, Shintoism, or Christianity. Thus we are now poised to argue that *Nihonjinron* is a religion.

## Civil Religion

Granted that BenDasan's *Nihonkyō* consists of a variety of uniquely Japanese cultural trappings of *Nihonjinron* sorts, in what sense is *Nihonjinron* a religion? In trying to answer this question, we look to the concept of civil religion, which for Japan has been enunciated most clearly by Robert Bellah and Winston Davis.

Let us start with a couple of definitions. Bellah states, 'By civil religion I refer to that religious dimension, found I think in the life of every people, through which it interprets its historical experience in the light of transcendent reality' (1975: 3). But civil religion is also 'the set of beliefs, rites and symbols which relates a man's role as citizen and his society's place in space, time, and history to the conditions of ultimate existence and meaning' (Coleman 1970: 70). To round out, we add here Davis's definition (1976: 6): civil religion is 'systematic network of moods, values, thoughts, rituals, and symbols that establishes the meaning of nationhood within an overarching hierarchy of significance.'

One salient feature of these and other definitions of civil religion is the idea that a political entity is the unit of common religious practice and that religious practices help endorse, validate, and legitimate the political entity through the individual's 'religious' practices. Note, for example, the term *civil* in 'civil religion,' Coleman's use of *citizen* in his definition, and Davis's use of *nationhood* in his. In Bellah's words, civil religion deals with 'the problem of legitimacy, which includes among other things, the question whether *existing political authority is moral and right or whether it violates higher religious duties*' (Bellah, 1980: viii, emphasis added).

In short, one of the fundamental questions of civil religion is whether a political entity such as a state is one undivided religious community. Is Japan a community of *Nihonkyō* faithful in Ben-Dasan's terms, or a 'civil-religious 'congregation' made up of a national consensus' represented by *Nihonjinron* in Davis's terms (1973: 325)? If *Nihonjinron* is Japan's civil religion, it is reasonable to regard it also as a manifestation of Japan's cultural nationalism. After all, nationalism is religion (Hayes 1926). As such, *Nihonjinron* is a prime candidate for the political religion of Japan in Apter's sense (1967) perhaps even more than Shintoism is.

## Civil Religion, American and Japanese

An additional salient feature of civil religion in America is what Richey and Jones (1974) call 'Protestant civic piety.' Similarly, Jones finds 'the origin of American civil religion…in the fusion of the American and Protestant historical traditions' (quoted in Gehrig 1981: 3). In a generic sense, 'civil piety' here resembles the civic piety in Japan before the end of the Pacific war. The theistic conception of the emperor in Japan was parallel to the theistic conception of a transcendental authority of the nation in America. Just as there was legitimation of Protestant values in America and integration of Protestant citizens as American, one can find in Japan legitimation of Shinto values and integration of Japanese subjects through Shinto. One thus might say that one source of Japanese civil religion can be found in the fusion of the Japanese and their Shinto historical traditions.

Japan's All Souls' Day (*O-bon*) and New Year's celebration, which are deeply rooted in Japan's folk religion, are as quin-tessentially Japanese as such holidays as the Fourth of July and Memorial Day are in America (Warner 1961). Also, although not a national celebration, a wedding in Japan is an expression of Japanese civil religion, not because it is sometimes conducted as a Shinto, Christian, or Buddhist rite, but because it embodies fundamental values of Japanese culture (Edwards 1989; Goldstein -Gidoni 1997).

As another variety of American civil religion Gehrig (1981: 3) discusses 'religious nationalism,' in which 'the nation itself is glorified and adored, becoming self-transcendent,' this is reminiscent of Apter's concept of 'political religion,' as elaborated by Davis (1973: 18–20). Pre-1945 Japan certainly exhibited religious nationalism, inasmuch as Shinto became an instrument of the state (Holtom 1943; Hardacre 1989) – a genuine case of 'state-sponsored civil religion' (Gehrig 1981: 81).

Coleman (1970: 70) names Martin Luther King Jr. and John F. Kennedy as saints of American civil religion. This parallels BenDasan's naming Saigō Takamori as a saint of *Nihonkyō*.

The integrative and legitimating functions of civil religion in America are advanced by advocates of the concept of American civil religion, such as Bellah and Coleman. The idea of the integrative function of religion goes back to Durkheim, of course. Durkheim's functional theory of religion, devised for Australian aboriginal and other societies with 'mechanical' solidarity, is here applied to more differentiated societies with 'organic' solidarity, such as Japan and America. The integrative and legitimating functions of *Nihonjinron* are obvious in the sense that *Nihonjinron* gives an unswerving definition of who the Japanese are, presenting a 'national consensus' to those who espouse it. The ethnocentric celebration of Japan's cultural tradition and values is tantamount to exhortation of worship of the society, precisely as Durkheim argued. Since the society and the nation are isomorphic in *Nihonjinron*, worship of the society is ipso facto worship of the nation.

## Bellah and Davis on Japanese Civil Religion

Bellah (1980) claims that civil religion has existed in Japan since the fifth or sixth century, regarding Prince Shōtoku's intentional introduction of Buddhism as a case of deliberate manipulation of civil religion.[23] According to Bellah, this intentional manipulation of civil religion by the state continues through modern times. Bellah's basic position was first laid down in his *Tokugawa Religion* (1957). In particular, Japan's emphasis on the role of particularism, the family, and the state as religio-political entities;

the priority of 'political' values; the role of benefaction-loyalty; and the absence of universal transcendence in Shinto propounded in this work presage his later views of the civil religion of Japan (Davis 1973: 298).

Bellah lets Watsuji Tetsurō, whom we encountered in past chapters, be the spokesman for Japan's pre-1945 civil religion. In addition to being an ecological *Nihonjinron* spokesman, Watsuji was a thoroughgoing supporter of the imperial institution. According to Bellah (1965: 590), 'Watsuji exalted the emperor system above all the religions and philosophies of the world and found it the highest form of human cultural expression,' and 'for all its sophistication Watsuji's theory is wholly committed to Japanese particularism.' Bellah continues (1965: 592):

> A crucial aspect of the problem of Japan's cultural identity is its profound resistance to the differentiation of the cultural system and correlatively to the differentiation of social system and personality...Individuals are defined fundamentally as group members and have no identity independent of the group...It is the experience of the Japanese collectivity structure, of the actually operative *kyodotai*, which lies at the root of these attitudes and makes them so persistent.

Though the emperor disappeared from the postwar Nihonjinron, as was discussed in the preceding chapter and will be in the next, he occupied the center stage of Nihonjinron until Japan's defeat in the Pacific war. We should also note that Bellah identifies the centrality of groupism and particularism in the pre-1945 Nihonjinron, a centrality that continues into the postwar era.

Davis's discussion of Japanese civil religion ranges over pre-1945 and postwar periods. For the pre-1945 period, he elaborates on the appropriation of the emperor and the mythification of the emperor through the use of *kojiki* and through the creation of state Shinto and 'shinto nationalism' (Davis 1976). As Bellah chose Watsuji as spokesman for the pre-1945 Japanese civil religion, Davis reconstructs civil religion of pre-1945 Japan through the analysis of Inoue Tetsujirō, a Tokyo University professor and one of the major civil theologians of the late Meiji–Taisho–early Showa period, who enjoyed enormous government favor and exerted considerable influence on the minds of the Japanese.

Inoue expounded on national morality based on 'the way of gods' and national polity (*kokutai*), always placing, as Watsuji did, the emperor in the central role. After the emperor, 'the most important elements that went into the making of the civil religion of modern Japan were precipitates of the religion of family and village' (Davis 1976: 35). Here, Davis echoes Bellah's analysis of Watsuji, in which the 'corporate group (*kyōdōtai*),' such as the family and the village community, was the focal point of pre-1945 Japanese civil religion.

Nationalism and civil religion alike are idealistic and utopian. Nationalism posits a state of affairs that is desired but not yet attained. Civil religion as a system of values, too, creates a normative orientation, an idealized worldview that members are expected to subscribe to and strive for. This is also precisely what *Nihonjinron* is. Davis puts it thus: 'Civil religion sets before a culture certain as-yet unattained goals while, at the same time, legitimating those goals already achieved' (Davis 1973: 32).

Davis turns his attention to postwar Japan in his analysis of 'Japan theory' – his term for *Nihonjinron* – in relation to civil religion (1983, 1992). Here Davis outlines *Nihonjinron* and describes it as a 'secularized' version of the pre-1945 Japanese civil religion. How is *Nihonjinron* related to civil religion? Let us turn our attention to this issue now.

## *Nihonkyō*, *Nihonjinron*, and Civil Religion

Does BenDasan's *Nihonkyō* add up to Japan's civil religion? Is it a civil religion at all? Or is *Nihonjinron* Japan's civil religion? And if so, in what way?

One thing is clear: BenDasan has identified 'the religion of Japan (*Nihonkyō*), which transcends individual religious affiliation. It is in short a religion common to all Japanese, in precisely the same way that American civil religion is supposedly common to all Americans regardless of religious faith. Thus Bellah says, 'We have had a Catholic president; it is conceivable that we could have a Jewish one' (1975: 183). Bellah is implying that the creed of American civil religion is able to embrace a president of any religious affiliation.

Drawing an analogy between certain practices in America and certain aspects of *Nihonkyō*, BenDasan says, '[In America] whether you are Christian, a Jew, or a Buddhist, all you have to do is to pledge allegiance to the flag of the United States. Then, it matters not what your faith is' (1975: 19). Here one sees how close BenDasan comes to conceptualizing civil religion in *Nihonkyō* without realizing it.

Japan abounds with civil religious expressions of a popular nature. Some of the most important with respect to the civil religion of Japan in the pre-1945 period were such symbols as the emperor, the national flag, and the national anthem, which identify Japan's nationhood. But any natural phenomenon or cultural product unique to Japan is a fair symbol of Japaneseness. Mt. Fuji, *geisha*, and cherry blossoms have been traditional symbols, now worn out and even somewhat tarnished, perhaps replaced by the bullet train, semiconductors, and personal audio headsets. Other symbols abound: jūdō, karate, kabuki, noh, *ikebana*, bonsai, *koto*, and *shamisen*, to which now we must add karaoke. To be sure, as discussed in earlier chapters, these or other symbols do not achieve 100 percent endorsement by the Japanese. Thus adherents of *Nihonkyō* are expected to number considerably less than the totality of the population. Nonetheless, the concept's reigning significance as the civil religion of Japan cannot be denied.

The role of Shinto should be considered in this connection. State Shinto played a pivotal role in constructing and maintaining Japan's civil religion before 1945, as Bellah (1965, 1980) and Davis (1973, 1976) both have extensively argued. But since the war, precisely because of the critical role it played before 1945, state Shinto has been officially banned (and unofficially relegated to pariah status in integrating the polity). Folk Shinto, on the other hand, is still alive and well half a century after the war, and now in some crucial respects takes up the space vacated by the retirement of state Shinto. Folk Shinto cannot take the political role that state Shinto played before 1945 when state Shinto was fused with the emperor system. But as the only indigenous religion of Japan and the only religion espoused exclusively by the Japanese, folk Shinto plays an indispensable role in both legitimating and integrating Japanese society and its polity.

As for civil religious rituals, I have mentioned the New Year's ritual, which is still carried on by vast numbers of families. To be sure, more and more Japanese are shunning the event by going abroad or at any rate taking a vacation away from home to avoid traditional visitations by relatives, friends, neighbors, and others, which are now seen to be more and more meaningless as well as excessively onerous and expensive. The midyear All Souls' Day (*O-bon*) continues to be a time of massive nationwide movement of people as they travel once a year from cities to rural homeland to reestablish the attenuated relationship between the urbanites who left the countryside generations ago and their few remaining rural relatives as a metaphor for reconnecting with their ancestors and with traditional Japan. Although such rituals are practiced in Korea and China, too, Japanese consider the rituals unique to the extent that they are unaware of similar practices in neighboring cultures and to the extent that these rituals have unique Japanese elements.

## Contestation of *Nihonjinron*

As I discussed in Chapter Five, the national flag, the national anthem, and the emperor system as symbolic components of Japanese civil religion are not totally accepted by all Japanese. They are problematic civil religious symbols in Japan because of their obvious past involvement in World War II. The war was fought in the name of the emperor. Soldiers died for him and civilians suffered because of him. The flag and the anthem were constant accompaniments of war efforts carried out in the name of the emperor. It is understandable, then, that each year around March or April, we learn from media reports of schools at which the national anthem was deliberately not sung and the national flag not flown in spite of the administrative guidance to do so from the Ministry of Education. Opposition to the Showa emperor's funeral and the current emperor's enthronement, though decidedly in a minor key in terms of scale and content, reverberated nationwide throughout the period of their preparation and execution.

But we should also remember that the imperial involvement with war is more and more forgotten, to the chagrin of liberals and antiestablishment elements, as the wartime generation dies off and postwar generations without war experience become the majority of the society. To a whole generation of young people these imperial involvements mean very little. During the funeral of the

Showa emperor and the enthronement of the present emperor, they did their best to kill their boredom, forced on them because all television stations focused on the event, by viewing rented video entertainment rather than participating in the events directly by joining the throng of onlookers or vicariously through the media (some – a small minority – took part in protest demonstrations).

Perhaps reflecting the disaffected segments and generations of the population, Manabe and I found in our 1987 questionnaire survey that a large percentage of Japanese do not subscribe to various tenets of *Nihonjinron*. Only 38 percent of the sample agreed that the Japanese are homogeneous people (*tan'itsu minzoku*). Although a smaller percentage of respondents (23 percent) disagreed, about as many people (39 percent) as those who agreed were undecided. Only 49 percent agreed that Japan was a unique culture; 42 percent could not make up their minds. Similarly, we found surprisingly low percentages, mostly less than 50 percent, agreeing with tenets of *Nihonjinron* having to do with the importance of 'Japanese blood' for producing essentialized Japanese cultural and physical features, the defining criteria of Japaneseness, the normative need to exclude foreigners from participating in Japanese society, and so on (Befu and Manabe 1998).

Given these facts, then, what can we say regarding the role of *Nihonjinron*-as-civil religion as providing national consensus? This is a feature Davis (1973: 24) speaks of as one of the 'specifications' of civil religion. How can *Nihonjinron* perform the function requisite of civil religion if less than half the population subscribe to the tenets of *Nihonjinron*?

What makes *Nihonjinron* Japan's civil religion is that, as I said in Chapter Five, no other body of discourse can claim any higher degree of consensus in Japan. As an overarching worldview of Japan, *Nihonjinron* has no rival. No other worldview of the Japanese society, culture, and nation has a wide enough acceptance to compete successfully with *Nihonjinron*. Thus *Nihonjinron* prevails by default. Even those who do not accept it are silenced by the lack of rival worldviews to subscribe to. Besides, *Nihonjinron* writers do their best to portray it as if it were the only worldview of the Japanese and espoused by all Japanese. Thus there is precious little debate over Japan's national identity in the sense of discursive competition among competing models, save some discussion on multiculturalism, which is, though increasing, still a minor trend.

*Nihonjinron* provides an ideal and an identity as civil religion is supposed to do (Davis 1973: 24). *Nihonjinron* is a veritable worldview in its comprehensiveness of coverage of all aspects of culture and history. Based as it is on revered values of the traditional past, it is seen as a state of affairs for which Japanese should strive in celebration of the status quo ante. Its principles are prescriptive exhortations of what Japanese should be and should do. They are, in short, prescriptions of the *Nihonjinron*-based civil religion of Japan.

Perhaps more than anything else, *Nihonjinron* provides the material for Japanese ethnic and national identity. In fact, it is no exaggeration to say that identity is the core of *Nihonjinron*. The goal of the whole enterprise of the *Nihonjinron* publishing industry is to provide a unique definition of who the Japanese are and what Japanese culture is.

In this connection, it is important to point out that among the criteria for being Japanese covered in the Nishinomiya survey, only Japanese citizenship was considered important by more than half the respondents, 71 percent agreeing (Befu and Manabe 1989). More than parentage, place of birth, place of socialization, patronym, and physical appearance, respondents considered citizenship to be by far the most important factor in defining Japaneseness. Inasmuch as no other criterion won more than 42 percent of the vote, if I may use those terms, 71 percent clearly indicates the importance of citizenship in defining Japaneseness in the minds of the Japanese.

This finding throws a new light on the nature of *Nihonjinron*, which one tends to think of in cultural terms, rather than as a political issue. Although cultural tenets exist and can not be ignored, the political component turns out to be most important in the minds of the Japanese. Seeing civil religion as a way of ratifying citizenship, then, *Nihonjinron*-as-civil religion is performing its function.

Given the conception of Japan – wherein the Japanese polity is coterminous with language, race, culture, and ethnicity – commitment to the belief in the symbolic sacredness of language, race, culture, and ethnic identity cannot help but enhance one's commitment to the polity of which these cultural trappings are symbolic manifestations. Belief in the uniqueness of the language, in the homogeneity of the race, in the purity of the culture, and in the exclusivity of the ethnic unit, then, heightens one's commitment to the polity. Any threat to the sociocultural boundary of the Japanese language, race, culture, and ethnicity, as Roy Andrew Miller argues (1982), is seen as a threat to the integrity of the polity. Defending and upholding language integrity, racial purity, and cultural uniqueness is then ipso facto defense of the national polity.

BenDasan's *Nihonkyō* can indeed be considered a civil religion, in spite of the fact that he himself is unaware of this fact and his exposition of *Nihonkyō* lacks systematization. When we treat his *Nihonkyō* as a species of *Nihonjinron*, or obversely consider *Nihonjinron* as part of his *Nihonkyō*, we see the blossoming of Japanese civil religion. When we add rituals and symbols, some with obvious religious ramifications, such as *O-bon*, and some without, such as the annual summer high school baseball tournament, we have Japanese civil religion in full bloom.

The legitimation of Japan's polity through *Nihonjinron*-as-civil religion is also saliently seen in the remarks made by Japanese political leaders. We are reminded of Prime Minister Nakasone's denigrating comments about racial and ethnic minorities in the United States and celebration in contrast of the supposedly homogeneous Japan, but he is hardly the only politician making similar comments about an America that cannot get its act together presumably because of its cultural heterogeneity and about the Japan that supposedly prospers because of its contrasting racial, social, and cultural homogeneity.

All these parts add up to a whole that constitutes the civil religion of Japan, in which *Nihonjinron* plays a major role, as it is wedded to Japan's polity to constitute Japan's civil religion. In pre-1945 modern Japan, there were well-established and numerous 'scriptures' of Japanese civil religion. The Imperial Rescript on Education, promulgated in 1890, must be nominated as the most important canon by anyone's standard. Exegesis of this canonical document appeared endlessly in pre-1945 Japan. The Imperial Rescript for Soldiers, supposedly memorized by every imperial soldier, is another. Davis nominates Inoue Tetsujirō's various writings (for example, Inoue 1891, 1912) as additional scriptural writings of *Nihonkyō*. After the Imperial Rescript on Education, *Kokutai no Hongi* (Principles of National Polity), drafted by the government and enunciating the official position on national polity, can easily be considered one of the most important scriptural writings of pre-1945 civil theology of Japan. Lesser works would include, for example, the morality (*shūshin*) texts used in schools. These writings and the philosophy behind them, then, constitute the civil theology of pre-1945 modern Japan.

What then of the civil theology of postwar Japan? The Imperial Rescript was banned after the war, and none of the other major scriptural writings survived. We now have innumerable tracts called *Nihonjinron* circulating in the market, with none emerging as a canonical work. One might say that *Nihonjinron* writers are the spiritual leaders of the postwar civil religion of Japan. They are the print equivalent of street corner preachers giving their idiosyncratic interpretations of the Bible on a soapbox, except that here 'the Bible' is not a written scripture but an imaginary state of what Japan should be like, the model *for* thought and action *for* the Japanese. To the extent that what they preach is secularized *Nihonjinron*, their teachings may be called the secular theology of Japan's civil religion.

If the imperial institution – as symbolized in the person of the emperor, the national flag, the national anthem, and the national emblem (the stylized chrysanthemum design), as constituted and propagated since Meiji – along with the tenets of *Nihonjinron*, may be regarded as a 'Japanese covenant,' then the postwar allergy, or resistance to and protest against the imperial institution and the inability to reach consensus regarding the tenets of *Nihonjinron* – witness the low percentage of people espousing *Nihonjinron* in our survey – may be thought of as a 'broken covenant,' precisely as Bellah (1975) feels with respect to America. If the Meiji Restoration was the first time of trial, and the defeat in World War II was the second, perhaps Japan is now facing its third time of trial, as the United States is now going through its third time of trial, according to Bellah – the first being the Revolutionary period; the second, the Civil War period; and the third, the present (Bellah 1970: 184).

How Japan's broken covenant is to be repaired is anyone's guess, of course. Proposals vary, and come from different political corners. The ultra-right wing would like to resuscitate the imperial institution in its old glory. But this position wins few hearts in Japan, and in fact causes most Japanese to shun ultranationalists. To the extreme left are those who would like to abolish the imperial institution. But this position, too, is not popular among very many Japanese. In the middle is a vast majority of relatively apolitical, inert though educated people who are willing to be manipulated by the government (Wolferen 1989, 2000). And the government is molding their minds through such means as control of education – witness textbook censorship and forcing of the national anthem and the national flag upon students. In the end, the imperial institution is most likely to continue. The death of the last emperor removed from the scene the prominent symbol of Japan's infamous actions in World War II. Too, as those who experienced the war and are most adamant and vociferous about their anti-imperial position die, so will the strong opposition, as grounded in the lived experiences of the war. The worldview based on *Nihonjinron* – or BenDasan's *Nihonkyō* – will be modified or relaxed in some respects, but will no doubt continue to receive the support of the establishment as a source of Japanese identity, in short, as Japan's civil religion, unless – and this is a big 'unless' – a rival civil religion can emerge to claim the hearts of the majority of Japanese. So far, none is on the horizon.

# 7 Geopolitics, Geoeconomics

We have examined the national and cultural identity located in Japan's traditional cultural repository, consisting of values, language, social institutions, and mental disposition. This *Nihonjinron* of the last three to four decades is stated in laudatory, sometimes even hawkish, terms. That which constitutes Japan's uniqueness, whether it be respect for harmony, group loyalty, implicit style of communication, or *mono no aware* as an esthetic ideal, is a source of pride for the Japanese.

The nature of Japan's identity, however, has not been the same throughout the recent history of Japan. In this chapter, I will deal with the complexity of differing identities of Japan in different periods of history. This brief review of the vicissitudes of Japan's identity discourse seeks their causes in geopolitical and geoeconomic factors. Strictly speaking, what I present in this chapter is not a history in the proper sense of the term but rather an analytical account of identity politics and the factors surrounding its development in different periods of Japanese history.[24]

Before we begin examining historical periods to see how identities of Japan unfold, however, we must review the operations of several processes. First, the contents of Japan's identity discourse is a function of the culture, nation, or civilization that Japan compares itself with. In the late Tokugawa period, *kokugaku* scholars constructed Japan's identity by contrasting Japan with China. Immediately after the Meiji Restoration, however, Japan's contrastive Other was the West, especially Europe. After World War II, the United States loomed large as Japan's Other at the expense of Europe.

A second important facet to remember is the pattern of vacillating views of the Japanese themselves, alternating between a positive, self-congratulatory construction of themselves on one hand and a negative, self-denigrating construction on the other.

One might call these 'positive cultural nationalism' and 'critical cultural nationalism,' respectively. We will see how these two entirely opposite discourses develop in succession.

A third important point examined in this chapter is that swings in identity discourse are prompted by geopolitical and geoeconomic factors. If such factors are favorable to Japan – such as victory in war or economic dominance – positive cultural nationalism prevails. Negative or critical cultural nationalism, on the other hand, is ushered in when Japan views itself as being inferior to the contrastive Other as in the case of loss of the Second World War or in the 'gunboat diplomacy' of the terminal Tokugawa period.

## Nascent Nativism of the Late Tokugawa Period

Understanding contemporary *Nihonjinron* and its historical lineage takes us back at least to the late Tokugawa, the feudal period at the turn of the nineteenth century. In this period, we already find clear and definite discussion of Japanese self-identity. We see budding *Nihonjinron*, though it was not called that in those days, in the National Learning school (*kokugaku*).

The National Learning scholarship arose in reaction against the received sinology of the time (Nosco 1990). Sinology, emphasizing neo-Confucianism, heavily influenced the feudal government in formulating the official political and moral philosophy. In contrast, National Learning scholars, such as Kamo no Mabuchi (1697–1769) and Motoori Norinaga (1730–1801), emphasized and lauded virtues that they considered to be pure, indigenous Japanese culture and institutions. The imperial institution was at the center, but Japan's aesthetic values, such as *mono no aware* (melancholic empathy with nature) and *yamato-gokoro* (the Japanese ethos) were important ingredients. In *Shōikō*, Mabuchi openly criticized the 'effeminate' China and in contrast raved about Japanese 'masculinity.' When Norinaga pointed to fragrant cherry blossoms seen against the rising sun as the essence of the ethos of Japan (*yamato-gokoro*), juxtaposing it with the ethos of China (*kara-gokoro*), he was staking a claim of a Japan totally different from China and of the superiority of Japanese culture over Chinese culture. Norinaga also declared in

*Kenkyojin* that the sun goddess, Amaterasu, stood at the pinnacle of the world.

It is important that Norinaga had studied neo-Confucianism, and his later specialization in *kokugaku* was due to his dissatisfaction with it.[25] Modern *Nihonjinron*, to the extent that it tries to prove Japan's superiority over the West, thus follows the example of *kokugaku* scholars in attempting to demonstrate the superiority of Japanese culture over its referent China.

The fundamental fault of the Tokugawa regime, as far as the National Learning school was concerned, was that centuries ago the Tokugawa shōgun displaced the emperor as the rightful sovereign ruler of the country. There was no way to rectify this situation except by toppling the Tokugawa regime and reinstating the imperial system, a primordial institution indigenous to Japan. For the National Learning school, Japan's highest virtues were to be sought in traditional Japan, by which is meant one unencumbered by any Chinese influence whatsoever. It made its mark by scoffing at and denigrating Chinese civilization and all that it represented. The hegemony of neo-Confucianism in Japanese polity was an unfortunate as well as erroneous twist in history from which Japan had to be rescued by putting indigenous institutions and values back in the center stage, where they rightfully belonged. The National Learning school thus provided a crucial ideological impetus for the political movement that led the impatient *shishi*, the 'samurai with purpose' of the National Learning persuasion, to topple the Tokugawa feudal regime and replace it with a government that held the emperor as its sovereign in 1868.

From the end of the eighteenth century, ships of Western powers began to appear off the coast of Japan, demanding the opening of its ports for trading. Hard as Japan tried to ward off 'hairy barbarians,' the guns on those boats, symbolizing Western military might, proved too much for the very best swords of Japan. After many unsuccessful battles and skirmishes, Commodore Perry's 1853 gunboat diplomacy in Tokyo Bay forced Japan to give up its self-imposed seclusion and to sign treaties with terms unfavorable to itself. The shame of this symbolic rape became a legacy indelibly imprinted on Japan, and defined one of the basic modes of identity discourse until the present time.

# The Auto-Orientalism of the Early Meiji Period

To come to terms with the military and technological gap with the West that Japan was forced to recognize, Meiji leaders ushered in a period of frenzied catch-up through borrowing and adaptation of Western technology and institutions in an effort to bring not only Japan's military strength but its political, economic, educational, and just about all other institutions up to par with the West.

This situation necessitated that Japan develop a definition of itself vis-à-vis the West. China was no longer a nation to contend with. Defining Japan as 'anti-China,' as of the National Learning scholars of the Tokugawa period did, was now an anachronism. The question 'Who are the Japanese?' became 'What makes Japan different from the West?' Japan turned 180 degrees – from facing China to facing Europe and the United States. Now Japan's identity had to contain elements to distinguish itself from the West.

During the second half of the nineteenth century, Fukuzawa Yukichi, Nishi Amane, and other intellectuals compared Japan with the West and argued the pros and cons of Japanese culture. Writing under a pseudonym, Fukuzawa contrasted the Japanese character with the Western character (Minami 1982: 116–117). Fukuzawa particularly despised what he regarded as outmoded feudal mentality among the Japanese and advocated radical changes to the Japanese way of life. This view was supported by a number of other intellectuals who belonged to a progressive organization called Meirokusha. Many others took Japanese traditional values and institutions to task, and some even advocated marriage with Europeans as a way of infusing 'Caucasian blood' to improve the Japanese race (Minami 1982: 25).

The overwhelming view of the time was that Japanese technology and social institutions were hopelessly outmoded and needed to be replaced by the more advanced Western technology and institutions. The zeal with which the Japanese absorbed Western civilization was phenomenal. It went far beyond guns and boats. Western costume was declared the official attire for government employees. Things of Western origin, whether food, shelter, or clothing, enjoyed high prestige. This infatuation with Western civilization ushered in the 'Rokumeikan period,' so called because of a Western-style society building called

Rokumeikan in the middle of Tokyo, where members of high society competed in displaying how Westernized they were, showing off their Western clothes and their skills in Western social manners and ballroom dancing.

The Japanese language, that sacrosanct store of the essence of Japanese spirit according to National Learning scholars, lost its raison d'être for some of the Meiji thinkers. According to Minami (1982: 110–111), Nishi Amane, one of the foremost thinkers of the time, advocated in 1874 using the English alphabet to record Japanese, foreshadowing a similar but more extreme proposal to be made by Mori Arinori, one of the intellectual leaders of the Meiji period and a one-time minister of education, who only a few years later suggested abolishing Japanese and replacing it with English.[26]

The Japanese did not arrive at their conclusions about Japanese society by themselves. Most Westerners who came to Japan to teach Western technology and to help build institutions modeled after those in the West – such as banking, the military, and education – regarded Japan as a backward country needing the enlightenment of the West. Western scientists, engineers, and scholars came to Japan in droves, taking high-paying salaries no Japanese of equivalent position could possibly command, and showed Japanese how to become modernized. That the Japanese government was willing to pay such high salaries to foreigners was in itself a blatant public admission of Japan's backwardness. In the end, however, cultural emulation of the West during the Meiji was superficial in many respects, the costume parties at Rokumeikan being a metaphor for the superficiality of the Western cultural cloak that Meiji socialites and elites wore (Uchida 1968).

I propose to call this process of self-denigration *auto-Orientalism*. One might call it 'do-it-to-yourself Orientalism.' It is a process of accepting the Orientalism of the West (Said 1978) by the very people who are being Orientalized. Psychologically a masochistic process, it signifies acceptance and internalization by the Orientalized people of the denigrated, racist definition given by Orientalizers. Said, of course, focused on the Middle East, but a similar Orientalizing process took place in other parts of the world, including Japan (Kang 1988; Minear 1980; Mouer 1983). In this process many Japanese intellectuals accepted the Western-centric scheme of the universe and embraced Westerners' value judgments about Japan's backwardness.

As far as basic human substance was concerned, however, the Japanese believed they had what it took spiritually to transform Japan into a modern nation. *Wakon yōsai*, meaning 'Japanese spirit, Western intellect,' was the motto of the day, appropriately modified from the older motto, *wakon kansai*, meaning 'Japanese spirit, Chinese intellect.' The West replaced China as Japan's role model.

But one cannot say that the discourse on national identity of the day had a mass following in the way *Nihonjinron* has now. Concern with Japan's identity vis-à-vis the West was a minor issue for the Japanese populace as a whole. It was primarily the few economically and politically powerful intellectuals – nevertheless those who made the difference for Japan's future – who concerned themselves with the issue of who the Japanese were. Historians of *Nihonjinron*, in discussing *Nihonjinron* before 1945, necessarily take up the small numbers of well-known writers and analyze their views. But for the vast majority of Japanese living in rural hinterlands, life was not much different from the feudal days, and the question of national identity occurred to them only when Japan engaged in wars. Of course, a sense of national identity was taught in schools then, and newspapers carried articles about Japan's role in international affairs. But most rural peasants were unconcerned with the question of who they were vis-à-vis Europeans.

We should not lose sight of the contrast in numbers and proportions of those engaged, actively or passively, in this identity discourse then and now. It was only after World War II that identity discourse became a concern of the masses. Until then, only a relatively small, though increasing, number of people was involved in this discourse.

It is important that from the beginning of Meiji, the West was permanently established as Japan's reference group, as the possessor of good things to emulate. The feeling of inferiority was firmly implanted as a result of the gunboat diplomacy in the last years of the Tokugawa period. Love and admiration of things Western came later. The term *hakurai*, meaning 'coming from abroad' but more specifically from the West, had a prestige value of its own. The slogan of the day, *bummei kaika*, meaning 'flowering of civilization,' referred to adopting trappings of Western civilization as a means of developing Japan. Love and admiration of the West continued as the manifest modus vivendi. Western culture was all-powerful, and Japanese culture represented backwardness and therefore was to be abandoned and forgotten.

## Return of Positive Identity

Yet one should not conclude that during the Meiji period the intellectual outlook was totally oriented toward degrading Japan.[27] Japan's nationalism continued in a minor key in the early Meiji period and became invigorated as time passed (Sakata Yoshio 1958). Perhaps partly in reaction to excessive Western devotion, periodicals like *Nihon* (1889–) and *Nihonjin* (1888–) began to appear in mid-Meiji, with the mission of reawakening the Japanese to uniquely Japanese characteristics and thereby bolstering the feeling of national pride and extolling Japanese virtues.

This position received a major boost in 1890 with the promulgation of the Imperial Rescript on Education, which officially defined the mythologically founded emperor system and outlined the fundamental principles that were to govern the Japanese educational system until the defeat of Japan in the Pacific war, crystallizing the pre-1945 pro-Japan discourse on the Japanese identity. This imperial message unquestionably remained the most influential document for propagation of the hegemonic ideology of the time and for officially defining Japanese identity. In it, the Japanese family system was presented as the embodiment of virtues and the foundation of the Japanese nation, wherein the emperor was the symbolic father of the subjects and filial piety was said to have created a social order unequaled around the world.

When the controversy erupted over whether foreigners should be allowed to live in Japan in intermingled residence with Japanese, Inoue Tetsujirō, mentioned in Chapter Six as one of the most passionate nationalists of the mid-Meiji, was moved to voice his opinion against the idea. He feared racial contamination, which, according to him, would result in loss of the ability of the Japanese to work together, in physiological alterations of the

Japanese, and possibly in the extinction of the Japanese race. This view was a 180-degree turnaround from the early Meiji view of advocating mixed marriage for the eugenic purpose of improving the Japanese race.

The Imperial Rescript on Education and also a good deal of *Nihonjinron* of the time contained many Confucian-derived ideas, such as the 'five principles' of human ethics. The Confucian analects were taught in schools, too, and assiduously memorized by schoolchildren. This amalgam of indigenous Japanese values and Confucian values may seem contradictory, if *Nihonjinron* were to identify Japanese values in contradistinction to any foreign value. What is important to remember, however, is that in Meiji the significant Other was no longer China but overwhelmingly the West. Thus incorporation of Chinese or Confucian values, especially as nativized by Japanese neo-Confucian scholars, was not seen as a problem in defining what constituted Japaneseness. At this point, distinguishing Japan from the West was what obsessed Japanese intellectuals. Whether in the process Chinese elements were mingled in the definition of Japaneseness was of little consequence.[28]

By the late Meiji, as Japan's industrialization proceeded successfully, and as Japan was slowly able to gain a stronger position vis-à-vis the West in diplomacy, trade issues, and military matters, an affirmative view of Japan began to hold sway. Japan was beginning its imperialist expansion into the continent and fighting back incursions by Western powers into East Asia. To rationalize Japan's action and to bolster Japanese morale, it was imperative to develop a national identity that made Japanese people feel proud of themselves. With the successive victories in the Sino-Japanese War of 1894–1895 and the Russo-Japanese War of 1904–1905, the Japanese people were in a mood to embrace such a self-definition. Although these wars crippled Japan's economy, the victories vastly enhanced Japan's international position. The improving self-image of Japan and the ascendancy of positive *Nihonjinron* should be seen in this geopolitical light.

One noteworthy development of this period was nationalization of folk Shinto (Hardacre 1989; Holtom 1943). To laud and praise the ethnic essence of Japan was to sacralize the emperor and the nation. There was no better way of accomplishing this objective than to co-opt indigenous folk Shinto. Since Shinto was quintessentially Japanese and embodied essentialized Japanliness, the Japanese state achieved an as yet higher degree of positive *Nihonjinron* by upgrading it to state religion and by placing the imperial institution at its center and formally organizing an innumerable number of hithertofore private folk Shinto shrines dotting the landscape of Japan into a hierarchy of state Shinto ecclesia. Because folk Shinto constituted an underpinning of *Nihonjinron*, appropriation of this *Nihonjinron*-in-private-sector for state purposes was a strategic move.

Shiga Shigekata, a political economist who frequently contributed to the magazine *Nihonjin* on Japan's economic policy, also wrote on uniquely Japanese characteristics. In creating his version of *Nihonjinron*, Shiga (See Ikumatsu ed. 1977) wrote a piece claiming Japan's natural scenery to be the most beautiful in the world, deriving from it a positively characterized Japanese personality. Miyake Setsurei (1977 [1891]) was more evenhanded in his view of the Japanese, enumerating both their seamy side and their laudable side. Miyake criticized Japan's 'feudal class structure' but he also lauded Japan's traditional culture. It is no surprise that Shiga as well as Miyake was a principal contributor to the right-wing nationalist magazine *Nihonjin* (Motoyama 1958).

Buoyed by the two successive victories, one against China and the other against Russia, intellectuals expressing positive views of Japan in the late Meiji era were legion, as elaborated upon by Minami (1994: 44–52). Ōmachi Keigetsu, to take one example, wrote a good deal on incomparable virtues of Japan, emphasizing the patriotism of the Japanese. He and many others saw Japanese virtues emanating from warrior ethics that developed in the preceding feudal period. In the area of esthetics (Minami 1982: 90), one might mention Kitamura Tōkoku, who elaborated on the esthetic value of *iki* in 1891, discussed in earlier chapters, of the plebeian culture that developed in the Tokugawa period, thus anticipating Kuki's classic study (1930) of the same concept. These views of Japan expressed by intellectuals are consonant with the manifest ideology that crystallized in the late Meiji (Gluck 1985; Pyle 1969). Kamishima calls this late Meiji period 'the first phase' of the Japanese concern with national identity (1990: 1).

## Taisho Interlude

During the so-called Taisho democracy, liberal thinking pervaded Japan. There were, to be sure, some like Tanaka Yoshitau (1924), who wrote a very successful nationalistic treatise, reprinted six times in three years, on 'national morality.' His writings are reminiscent of Inoue Tetsujirō's in that the Imperial Rescript on Education is the centerpiece of his argument about 'human conduct,' which according to Tanaka has to do with Shinto, the code of the warrior (*bushidō*), familism, and loyalty to the nation.

But basically the Taisho period did not promise, promote, or encourage strong continuation of *Nihonjinron*. Virtually all of the thousands of foreign engineers, technicians, and scholars brought over to create a Westernized Japan had been sent back by the end of Meiji. This was a time of relative peace in Japan. The liberalism of the Taisho period was no longer obsessed with wholesale and uncritical absorption of Western culture; it was more reflective and selective, assessing and evaluating things Western before importing them.

At the same time, Western thought actually began to take root at last, rather than merely floating on the surface and giving the appearance of enlightenment and progressivism without substance as in the Meiji period. Thus there was little room for staunchly nationalistic *Nihonjinron* to hold sway. Kamishima's periodicization of *Nihonjinron*, though he does not call it that, in fact skips the whole Taisho era and begins the second phase in the early Showa (1990: 1).

## Ultranationalism of the 1930s to 1945

It is in the 1930s, as Japan began its renewed effort to occupy and control much of East and Southeast Asia by removing Western powers occupying the area, that we see the resurgence of patriotic *Nihonjinron* of the basic variety characteristic of the late Meiji period. As Gluck (1985) says, Meiji ideologues laid the foundation of the political thinking that was to continue until 1945. Self-praise, often in the form of unqualified xenophobic ethnocentrism, increased in the 1930s when frenzied claims began to be made of the superiority of the Japanese in comparison with Europeans and Americans.

It was in the early Showa that Watsuji wrote his *Fūdo*, which sees an inextricable relationship between Japan's environment and its culture. As Minami (1982) notes, this publication was precipitated by the rise of Marxism. It was to be an answer to Marxism to demonstrate the impossibility of accounting for Japanese culture in the framework of historical materialism.

Shortly before, Kuki (1930), resuscitating Kitamura Tōkoku's argument but further enhancing it, wrote his well-known treatise on the concept of *iki* as representing the quintessential esthetic value of the Tokugawa plebeian Japanese. Shirayanagi Shūko (1938) followed Watsuji, arguing that the Japanese environment was the best and most desirable in the world and was even responsible for creating a uniquely Japanese genetic lineage. Note here the conflation of environment, culture, and biology whose legacy continues to this day. Seen in this increasingly jingoistic light, it is quite understandable that even Nishida Kitarō (1940), renowned Kyoto University professor and arguably the best philosopher Japan has ever produced, had succumbed to jingoism and joined the ranks of patriotic Nihonjinron writers.

Kōyama Iwao (1941), another scholar of the Kyoto school, developed a cultural taxonomy reminiscent of Watsuji's climatic classification. Predictably his *Nihonjinron* is almost a replica of Watsuji's in many respects, deriving from the environment Japanese personal character, aesthetics, and patriotism. Like Watsuji, Kōyama emphasized the emperor system as the hallmark of Japanese polity and claimed it to be unique in the world, calling Japan a divine nation. It was the uniquely superior character of the Japanese that was going to bring about the inevitable victory of Japan.

If the Imperial Rescript on Education was the most canonical of all canons of *Nihonjinron* before 1945, *Kokutai no Hongi* (The Essence of Japanese Polity), issued by the Ministry of Education in 1937 and distributed in large qualities, was a follow-up canon of the war period. Numerous versions of its commentary were published and reprinted to meet the high demand. This document elaborated on the centrality of the imperial institution and the superiority of Japan over its real and imagined allies and enemies in Asia and the West. Its intent was to convince the Japanese people of Japan's 'inevitable military victory.' It thus set the ideological stage for rationalizing the invasion of East Asia and the establishment of the Greater East Asia Co-Prosperity Sphere.

On another front, even Hasegawa Nyozekan, that spokesman of Taisho liberalism, extolled what he argued to be specifically 'Japanly' virtues (1938). His argument is reminiscent of Watsuji's ecological theory, starting with the supposed effect of the geography of Japan upon its culture and extending into lifestyle, human relations, and art.

But even more surprising is the suasion of Uchimura Kanzō, one of the greatest Japanese Christians, who was also moved to discuss the essence of Japaneseness in *Nihonjinron* terms through certain well-chosen 'representative' Japanese (Uchimura 1941). This work was a timely reissue in paperback of a translation of a book originally published in English in 1908 as *Representative Men of Japan* – timely, in that Japan was to enter the Pacific war in a few months, and therefore demonstration of 'Japanliness' to the Japanese people was needed more urgently than ever. This timely book's timelessness is demonstrated by the fact that it is still being reprinted – sixty years after it first appeared – on the average of once a year.

Uchimura chose the following individuals as representing the best qualities of the Japanese: Saigō Takamori, a tragic hero of the Meiji Restoration, who was forced to rebel against the government and commit suicide; Uesugi Kenzan, a feudal lord who ruled his domain with skill and benevolence in the late eighteenth and early nineteenth centuries; Ninomiya Sontoku, the agrarian philosopher and administrator of the same period; Nakae Tōju, a country Confucian teacher of the seventeenth century whose fame pervaded the country; and Nichiren of the thirteenth century, who founded the nationalistic Nichiren sect. This method of merely enumerating individuals is reminiscent of that used in numerous books titled *Nihon no Kokoro* or *Nihonjin no Kokoro* reviewed in Chapter Two and Chapter Three. It is highly instructive that Uchimura, a Christian, included a Buddhist priest to demonstrate what it takes to be a Japanese. It goes on to show the Japanization of Christianity in Uchimura. This fact is highly instructive in light of BenDasan's theory of all-encompassing *Nihonkyō*, which makes Uchimura merely a Christian sectarian of *Nihonkyō*.

*Nihonjinron* in one form or another became part of official ideology in the period from the Meiji Restoration to the end of World War II, waxing and waning in importance. The government used every means possible to propagate this worldview, including military and educational institutions and the media. This effort reached its height during the Pacific war. And the bloated view that Japan in every respect was superior to the rest of the world continued until it burst in August 1945.

## Postwar Auto-Orientalism

In the immediate postwar era, disastrous defeat in the Pacific War meant not only military defeat but total undermining of Japanese cultural values. For at least a decade – perhaps two decades – after 1945, Japan was in a period of depressing soul-searching. With the nation vanquished, the idealized *Nihonjinron* valorizing traditional values now seemed bankrupt. If such values were worth anything, why did Japan lose the war? The Japanese people had been promised victory by virtue of Japan's superior culture, but instead, this culture led Japan to unconditional surrender. Traditional Japanese values and institutions, which were mobilized for fighting the war, were now all objects of criticism. *Feudalistic*, *premodern*, *outmoded*, and *backward* were some of the epithets constantly thrown at whatever represented old and traditional Japan. The Marxist term *Asiatic stagnation* was also freely bandied about to define whatever institution was undemocratic, traditional, or contrary to the values – American, by and large – now held in high esteem. This self-castigation was as pervasive as it was thoroughgoing. Noted intellectuals such as Fukutake Tadashi, Hani Gorō, Inoue Kiyoshi, Ishimoda Tadashi, Kawashima Takeyoshi, Maruyama Masao, and numerous others rode the now fashionable bandwagon of self-blame, penning their pieces in the widely respected magazines for the intelligentsia, such as *Chūō Kōron* and *Bungei Shunjū*. Even Prince Takamatsu had to decree the Japanese family system 'feudalistic.'

Indeed, as we saw in Chapter Five, in the minds of many, even the legitimacy and the prestige of the emperor system were now in doubt. After all, right at the start of the occupation of Japan, the emperor himself made a trip to the headquarters of General Douglas MacArthur, the Supreme Commander of the Allied Powers, to pay homage. Alas, the divine emperor did not have the authority or power to summon MacArthur to the imperial palace for an audience. Newspapers carried on the front page a large picture of the diminutive emperor, dwarfed by the six-foot-tall MacArthur, leader of the Occupation forces, symbolizing the power relationship between the two. The emperor was no longer the kingpin of the Japanese polity. The imperial institution with its mythic foundation and national ideology and symbolism, all of which were marshaled forth for the war effort and constituted the core of *Nihonjinron*, well nigh lost their venerable and revered status. MacArthur, people said in jest, was the real emperor of Japan.

The Japanese family system was now to be condemned for its feudal character, as argued in the influential writings of Kawashima Takeyoshi (1950, 1957), the leading sociologist of law of the time. The normative values of *on* and *giri* likewise were given negative scores. Japan's traditional virtues all were cast as vices. Before and during the war, wartime propagandists contrasted democracy and individualism of the West with Japanese values and denigrated the former as worthless. But with the military reversal came a reversal of this position: democracy was now in and Japanese institutions that contrasted with and contradicted democracy were out because the latter had caused the defeat, according to the now-fashionable postwar interpretation.

Even the Japanese language, the supposed storehouse of Japanese values and virtues according to wartime and prewar *Nihonjinron* advocates from Motoori Norinaga on, came under attack: Japanese affords no logical discourse, according to its critics, as European languages presumably do. It enables discourse in feeling and emotion only. Shiga Naoya, a prominent writer who was called 'a god of Japanese belles lettres' for his literary facility, in 1946 even went so far as to propose abolishing Japanese and replacing it with another language like French, thus resuscitating Mori Arinori's suggestion of fifty years earlier (Miller 1982: 109–110). It was one thing for Occupation personnel to declare the inutility of Japanese, as they were wont to do. It was totally another for a notable Japanese intellectual who made his living with his pen to advocate such an auto-Orientalizing position. The wholesale castigation of traditional values was about as thorough as the total praise of them during the war.

In this situation, the discourse on Japan's identity of the late 1940s and the 1950s became one of comparing Japan with the West, especially the United States, the foe that vanquished Japan, as Japan's way of convincing itself how wrong it was. The West was held up as the model and the ideal, and whatever the West had and Japan did not have was the reason for Japan's defeat, as well as whatever the West did not have and Japan had. The example was set by Ruth Benedict, who – in *The Chrysanthemum and the Sword* (1946) – pronounced Japanese culture dead, according to Douglas Lummis (1981). Because it was written by an American, *The Chrysanthemum and the Sword* is not an example of discourse on Japan's self-identity. However, the book was read in translation by millions of Japanese almost as a revelatory truth about themselves. Legions of other Western observers, including MacArthur (who claimed that the Japanese had the mentality of a twelve-year-old), saw and analyzed Japan against the mirror of their own social values and in their naive ethnocentrism denigrated everything Japanese. Japanese intellectuals, tired of war and ashamed of the defeat, were delighted to have their newfound auto-Orientalism validated by observers from countries that represented a superior civilization and the new model for Japan.

Such auto-Orientalism was rampant as the defining mode of Japan's identity. A few examples will suffice. Tanikawa Tetsuzō, who taught at Hosei University and was associate director of a national museum at the time, criticized the Japanese national character in *Bunkaron* (1947) on several grounds. For one, in contrast to Christianity, which seeks salvation of the soul, Japanese mythology emphasizes hierarchical human relations and merely teaches obedience to authority. Second, this same mythology was responsible for the tendency to place the interest of the nation-state above the interest of the individual. Third, the Japanese do not know how to exercise freedom correctly. Fourth, the Japanese lack respect for the individual. In short, he criticized the Japanese for not possessing values commonly accepted as Western.

The burden of the feudal legacy on Japan's ills was repeatedly pointed out in this postwar period. In 1951, with a grant from

UNESCO, Japanese social scientists conducted a series of field researches on social tension. In the concluding roundtable discussion, Suzuki Jirō (then a sociologist at Tokyo Metropolitan University), who investigated the *burakumin* outcast minority, blamed the Tokugawa feudal system for the formation of the *burakumin* system (Nihon Jimbun Kagakkai 1953: 464). Toyota Takeshi, professor at Tohoku University, suggested in the same report that Japan was experiencing social tension because it was in transition from feudal to modern society.

This self-castigation – blaming Japan's tradition for Japan's misery – went hand in hand with the Occupation's pronouncement that virtually everything in Japan was antidemocratic and outmoded, and had to be reformed. The Japanese accepted the Occupation's verdict that the West was best and Japan was its opposite. Thus, for the second time in history, Japan went through a major period of auto-Orientalism.

It is in this context that we can comprehend the publication of one of the strangest works of sadomasochistic science fiction, *Kachikujin Yapū*, subtitled 'Yapoo, the Domesticated Cattle,' which, originally serialized in *Kidan Kurabu* starting in 1961, was authored by a certain Numa Shōzō (1991a, 1991b), a pseudonym presumably for Kurata Takuji, a Tokyo Superior Court judge. The novel takes place in the twenty-first century, when the white race finally conquers the universe and establishes an intergalactic empire.

The white race obliterates all the yellow races, except the Yapoo – the name being presumably derived from 'Japanese' – who are allowed to live, but only as a subhuman species, previous classification of the Yapoo as human having been found to be a taxonomic error. The Yapoo's only purpose is to serve the white race in myriad ways. Surgery is performed, for example, on some Yapoo to elongate the mouth to fit the genitals of the white masters and thus enable them more readily to swallow the urine and eat feces of their white masters without dripping. A white master's urine was considered to be 'divine aqua,' whose taste was unequaled by any other beverage. The Yapoo considered their masters' feces the most delectable of all foods and thanked God for the privilege of being allowed to partake of that feast. The tongues of some of them were surgically elongated to provide maximum sexual stimulation for their female masters. Genetic engineering created a whole variety of subspecies of Yapoo to serve different purposes, such as carrying their white masters on their backs, squatting to become living chairs for the white masters, and so on. One subspecies was created to provide the most delicious meat for the white race.

The story is probably the ultimate of self-denigration – auto-Orientalism at its extreme. It was born of the author's reaction to Japan's defeat, as he tells in the postscript of the book: he was ashamed of his country, which surrendered unconditionally, and ashamed of the ugly sight of the emperor standing next to General MacArthur in the photograph published in the newspapers immediately after the war (Numa 1991b: 654). This sense of shame then was expressed in creating a world in which the Japanese were totally subjugated by the white race and enthralled by their own subjugated status. That a story of this sort could be published indicates the extent to which the Japanese were under an auto-Orientalizing spell.

## Ascendancy of Positive Cultural Nationalism

It was not until the late 1960s that the balance began to tip and the Japanese began to see themselves in a positive light. By this time, the postwar 'allergy,' as this defeatist, auto-Orientalizing attitude was sometimes called, slowly began to be outweighed by a more self-confident, self-congratulatory identity.

As the postwar economy began to take off and enter the stage of rapid growth in the 1960s, the Japanese slowly regained self-confidence. *Nihonjinron*, too, began to take a turn and to portray Japan in a more favorable light. The self-same social institutions and the self-same cultural values that were objects of condemnation in the immediate postwar years were now seen to have positive valence: if they were not any better than those of the West, at least they were just as good. The Japanese were now finally able to take the cultural relativist position, rather than accepting uncritically and in toto the victor's value judgments (Aoki 1990).

Slowly regaining self-confidence, the Japanese began to marvel at their own phenomenal economic development and to see it as a result of or as fostered by Japan's unique social institutions, cultural values, and personality rather than as resulting *in spite of* Japan's 'premodern' or 'feudalistic' institutions and values. The overwhelming majority of *Nihonjinron* literature in the 1970s began to discuss the unique characteristics of Japan as its strength and the basis of Japan's global economic success. In the most recent period, the definition of Japanese cultural and national identity has even been imbued with ethnocentrism, seeing positive values in Japanese culture while denigrating the West.

A negative Japan and a positive Japan coexisted as uneasy bedfellows during the 1960s and 1970s. Critical or negative *Nihonjinron* held sway early in this period, but it was slowly overshadowed by a more positive *Nihonjinron*. From the late 1970s on, the vast majority of *Nihonjinron* literature began to discuss the unique characteristics of Japan as its strength and as the basis of its economic success, and even propounded the *Nihonjinron* thesis as Japan's prime mover.

Although the nature of the present-day *Nihonjinron* is so similar to the pre-1945 version, two glaring differences must be noted. One is the total absence even of mention of the emperor and the imperial institution as an accouterment of the postwar *Nihonjinron*. The other factor differentiating the contemporary period from the wartime and earlier situations is the level of state involvement. There is no overt state suppression of contrary views, at least not the sort that the infamous secret police executed during World War II, yet the kind of negative identity that prevailed in the immediate postwar era is well-nigh gone. Similarly, the Japanese who are embracing the view of 'Japan as Number One' because of its unique qualities are doing so without obvious state coercion. Forces of suasion are more subtle and indirect. In this respect, the contemporary positive evaluation of Japan, emanating from the grass roots, may perhaps be a stronger, more firmly rooted affair than the wartime *Nihonjinron*, which was supported by the state apparatus. For those who believe that contemporary *Nihonjinron* leads to narrow nationalism, conservatism, and rejection of a cosmopolitan outlook, this contemporary trend may be something to worry about.

Of late Japan's self-confidence has reached a new hawkish height, wherein Japan is represented as a country ready to take on the West and win. In thirty years' time the Japan that produced

*Yapoo*, that grotesquely auto-Orientalizing fiction, turned 180 degrees around and, now armed with positive cultural nationalism that is the current *Nihonjinron*, is poised to take on the world. The economic downturn since the early 1990s has dampened the Japanese confidence to some extent, but not enough to make a major modification in the role of Japan in the world scene and hence in the nature of *Nihonjinron*.

Current *Nihonjinron*, then, must be seen against the background of Japan's strong economic position worldwide. How long the positive self-view will continue will depend on Japan's geo-economic and geopolitical strength relative to world economic powers, notably the United States, but now also increasingly relative to other Asian powers, notably China. Will there be another era, in the twenty-first century, when Japan will define itself as 'anti-China,' as the National Learning School did in the first half of the nineteenth century? Only the future will tell us.

# Notes

1 For the Japanese versions, see Nakane (1967), Doi (1971), Watsuji (1935), D. Suzuki (1940), and BenDasan (1970).

2 BenDasan and Yamamoto seem are one and the same person, a point I return to in Chapter Six.

3 See Lee (1982a, 1982b, 1984) for a more recent statement on Japanese miniaturization.

4 One of the major criticisms of the group model is its essentialism, which stereotypes and reifies 'The Japanese' (Befu 1980, Mouer and Sugimoto 1986). Although this essentialism is just about laid to rest in anthropology and sociology, the issue has been resurrected in the academic field of psychology by Kitayama Shinobu of Kyoto University (see Kitayama, Markus, Matsumoto, and Norasakkunkit 1997 and Markus and Kitayama 1991 for argument in English). To Kitayama and his associates' essentialist argument, Takano Yōtarō and his associates (Takano and Ōsaka 1997, 1999) have fought back, faulting uncritical use of evidence by Kitayama's group. This debate in professional psychology is likely to continue for some time in the future.

5 For an English exposition of this concept, see Hamaguchi 1985.

6 Some of the books reviewed here are not the inexpensive paperbacks in which most *Nihonjinron* offerings are published; but these views are also published in other sources more accessible to the public, such as in newspapers and magazines. An annual special issue on management of the popular magazine *Bungei Shunjū*, for example, regularly carries articles by many of the management specialists cited here.

7 See Johnson (1993) for an excellent assessment of Doi's work.

8 For a recent exposition of the concept of *wabi* in English, especially in relation to the art of tea, see Tornianen (2000).

9   See Kindaichi (1978) for an English version of his treatise.

10  The questionnaire, designed to investigate respondents'
    knowledge about *Nihonjinron* and attitudes toward it, was
    sent to a random sample of 2,400 adults, of whom 39.8
    percent responded.

11  See Ishida (1974) for an English version.

12  I say 'a minimum of' because the publisher has no data on
    the number of printings for five of the earlier editions, and to
    be conservative I am counting these editions as having had
    one printing. More likely they, too, each produced numerous
    printings, probably more than later editions, since books tend
    to sell the most copies in the first few years of publication.

13  They are, in order of popularity: Edwin O. Reischauer (41
    percent), Aida Yūji (40 percent), Herman Kahn (33 percent),
    Isiah BenDasan (31 percent), and Donald Keene (28 percent).

14  BenDasan's *Nihonjin to Yudayajin* (21 percent), Benedict's
    *Kiku to Katana* (14 percent), and Doi's *'Amae' no Kōzō* (11
    percent). Nakane's well-known *Tate Shakai no Ningen
    Kankei* had been read by only 7 percent of the respondents.

15  Most comparisons of Japan with Asian cultures are done
    by Koreans, Chinese, and other non-Japanese Asians,
    rather than by Japanese themselves, for example, Kim
    (1983) and Lee (1982a; for English versions, see 1982b,
    1984) comparing Japan with Korea and Chin (1971) with
    China.

16  Watanabe's theory has nothing to do with the well-known
    equestrian hypothesis of Egami (1967), discussed in Chapter
    Two.

17  Incidentally, Watanabe assures us that an agricultural type
    society need not engage in agriculture, even though it
    presumably has its origins in agriculture. Similarly, a
    horseback-rider type society need not have any member
    riding horseback. This term merely implies certain traits,
    such as efficiency.

18  Buddhism, since it is shared among many Asian nations,
    cannot readily serve as a basis of nationalism in the same way
    Japan's native religion, Shintoism, can. Nichiren, to be sure,
    gave Buddhism a unique nationalistic interpretation. The
    Nichiren sect became militantly nationalistic and assumed a

role as protector of Japan at the time of the Mongols' attempted invasions in the thirteenth century.

19   The English translation was provided by the Asia Foundation Translation Service Center and appeared in the March 17, 1989, issue of the *Pacific Citizen*.

20   For details surrounding passage of this bill, see Itoh (2000).

21   Its 'translation,' *The Japanese and the Jews*, by Richard L. Gage (BenDasan 1972) is actually not a very faithful translation, as Gage himself admits. Some sections are more or less word-for-word translations, but some are liberal paraphrasing of the original, and some original sections simply are omitted.

22   In *The Japanese and the Jews*, the English version of *Nihonjin to Yudayajin*, *Nihonkyō* is translated as *Nihonism*, which does not quite carry the connotation of *Nihonkyō* specifically as a religion. The English suffix *-ism* is used for secular ideologies as well, such as Marxism or humanism, whereas in Japanese *-kyō* is never used in reference to a secular teaching, for which *-shugi* or *-ron* is a more likely choice. The suffix *-kyō*, on the other hand, is always associated with religion, such as *Buk-kyō* (Buddhism) or *Kirisuto-kyō* (Christianity). Thus *Nihonism* erroneously gives the connotation of a secular, nationalistic dogma. For this reason I shall continue to use the term *Nihonkyō*.

23   I rely heavily on Winston Davis (1973: chaps. 1 and 8) for my comments on Bellah in this section.

24   For the history of *Nihonjinron* see Aoki (1990), Ikumatsu (1963), and Minami (1982, 1994).

25   Norinaga reminds one of Watsuji Tetsurō, who a hundred years later (after returning from his study of Western philosophy in Germany) was to write *Fūdo* (1935) in reaction to Western philosophers' theory of the relationship between nature and human beings.

26   See Miller (1982: 107–109) for the circumstances surrounding this suggestion.

27   Ideological development of the mid- to late Meiji period, with all its complexity, is treated with great analytical skill by Gluck (1985) and Pyle (1969). What follows is a brief discussion of the highlights of what took place at this time.

28  This is a point that Dale (1986: 59–60) misses in his critique
     of *Nihonjinron*.

# References

Abegglen, James. (1958) *The Japanese Factory: Aspects of Its Social Organization*. Boston: MIT Press.

Aida, Yūji. (1976) *Nihonjinron no tameni* (On behalf of Nihonjinron). Tokyo: Ushio Shuppansha.

......... (1980) *Nihon no Fūdo to Bunka* (Environment and culture in Japan). Tokyo: Kōdansha.

Aizawa, Hisashi. (1976) *Nihonjinron no tameni* (On behalf of *Nihonjinron*). Tokyo: Ushio Shuppansha.

Amino, Yoshihiko. (1982) *Higashi to Nishi no Kataru Nihonshi* (The Japanese history from East and West). Tokyo: Soshiete.

......... (2000) *Nihon towa Nanika* (What is Japan?). Tokyo: Kōdansha.

Anderson, Benedict. (1983) *Imagined Communities*. London: Verso.

Anonymous. (1984, May) 'Hinomaru "100%" no naka de' (In the midst of 100% Hinomaru). *Sekai*, pp. 208–209.

Anzu, Motohiko. (1972) *Kokki no Rekishi* (The history of the national flag). Tokyo: Ōfūsha.

Aoki, Tamotsu. (1989a, June) 'Sengo Nihon to "Nihon bunkaron"' (Postwar Japan and *Nihonjinron*), Part 1. *Chūō Kōron*, pp. 156–173.

......... (1989b, July) 'Sengo Nihon to "Nihon bunkaron"' (Postwar Japan and *Nihonjinron*), Part 2. *Chūō Kōron*, pp. 158–183.

......... (1990) *Nihon Bunkaron no Hen'yō: Sengo Nihon no Bunka to Aidentitī* (Changes in *Nihonjinron*: Postwar culture and identity). Tokyo: Chūō Kōronsha.

Aoki, Tamotsu, et al., eds. (1999–) *Kindai Nihon Bunkaron* (Modern *Nihonjinron*). 11 vols. Tokyo: Iwanami Shoten.

Apter, David. (1967) 'Political Religion in the New States.' In *Old Societies and New States*, ed. Clifford Geertz. New York: Free Press, pp. 57–104.

Araki, Hiroyuki. (1973) *Nihonjin no Kōdō Yōshiki* (Behavior patterns of the Japanese). Tokyo: Kōdansha.

Aruga, Kizaemon. (1976) *Hitotsu no Nihon Bunkaron* (A certain *Nihonjinron*). Tokyo: Miraisha.

Ayabe, Tsuneo, ed. (1992) *Sotokara Mita Nihonjin: Nihonkan no Kōzō*(The Japanese as seen from outside: Views on the Japanese). Tokyo: Asahi Shinbunsha.

Ballon, Robert J. (1968) 'Japan's Lifelong Remuneration System.' *Industrial Relations Section Bulletin* 16. Tokyo: Sophia University.

Befu, Harumi. (1980) 'The Group Model of Japanese Society: A Critique.' In *Japanese Society: Reappraisals and New Directions*, eds. R. Mouer and Y. Sugimoto. *Social Analysis* (special issue), 5/6: 29–43.

......... (1983) 'Japan's Internationalization and *Nihon Bunkaron*.' In *The Challenge of Japan's Internationalization: Organization and Culture*, eds. H. Mannari and H. Befu. Nishinomiya: Kwansei Gakuin University, pp. 232–266.

......... (1990) 'Four Models of Japanese Society and Their Relevance to Conflict.' In *Japanese Models of Conflict Resolution*, eds. S. N. Eisenstadt and E. Ben-Ari. London: Kegan Paul International, pp. 213–238.

......... (1993) 'Nationalism and *Nihonjinron*.' In *Cultural Nationalism in East Asia*, ed. H. Befu. Berkeley: University of California Institute for East Asian Studies, pp. 107–135.

......... (1997) (*Zōho Kaitei*) *Ideorogī to shite no Nihon Bunkaron* ([Enlarged and revised] *Nihonjinron* as an ideology). Tokyo: Shisō no Kagakusha.

Befu, Harumi, and Kazufumi Manabe. (1989) 'An Empirical Investigation of *Nihonjinron*: The Degree of Exposure of Japanese to *Nihonjinron* Propositions and the Functions These Propositions Serve.' *Kwansei Gakuin University Annual Studies*, XXXVIII: 35–62.

......... (1991) '*Nihonjinron*: The Discursive Manifestation of Cultural Nationalism.' *Kwansei Gakuin University Annual Studies*, XXXX: 101–115.

......... (1998) 'Japanese Identity Statistically Profiled.' *Kwansei Gakuin University Sociology Department Studies* 79: 133–145.

Bellah, Robert N. (1957) *Tokugawa Religion*. New York: Free Press.

......... (1965) 'Japan's Cultural Identity: Some Reflections on the Work of Watsuji Tetsurō.' *Journal of Asian Studies*, 24: 573–594.

......... (1968) 'Shinto and Modernization.' In *Continuity and Change* (Proceedings of the Second International Conference for Shinto Studies). Tokyo: Kokugakuin University, pp. 158–162.

......... (1970) *Beyond Belief.* New York: Harper & Row.

......... (1975) *Broken Covenant: American Civil Religion in Time of Trial.* New York: Seaby Press.

......... (1980) 'Introduction.' In *Varieties of Civil Religion*, eds. R. N. Bellah and P. E. Hammond. New York: Harper & Row, pp. vii–xv.

Ben-Ari, Eyal. (2000) '"Global Talk"? Discourse and Cognition Among Japanese Business Managers in Singapore.' In *Japan in Singapore: Cultural Occurrences and Cultural Flows*, eds. E. Ben-Ari and J. Clammer. Richmond, Surry: Curzon, pp. 37–62.

BenDasan, Isaiah. (1970) *Nihonjin to Yudayajin* (The Japanese and the Jews). Tokyo: Yamamoto Shoten.

......... (1972) *The Japanese and the Jews.* New York: Weatherhill.

......... (1975) *Nihonkyō ni tsuite* (On *Nihonkyō*). Tokyo: Bungei Shunjū.

......... (1976) *Nihonkyōto: Sono Kaiso to Gendai Chishikijin* (*Nihonkyō* believers: The founder and modern intellectuals). Tokyo: Kadokawa Shoten.

Benedict, Ruth. (1946) *The Chrysanthemum and the Sword.* Boston: Houghton Mifflin.

......... (1948) *Kiku to Katana* (The chrysanthemum and the sword). Tokyo: Shakai Shisōsha.

Berque, Augustin. (1988) *Fūdo no Nihon: Shizen to bunka no tsutai* (Japan and its environment: The relationship between nature and culture). Tokyo: Chikuma Shobō.

Besshi, Atsuhiko. (1999) *Sekai no Kyōkasho wa Nihon o dō Oshiete Iruka* (How do textbooks of the world teach about Japan?). Tokyo: Asahi Shinbunsha.

Brown, William. (1966) 'The Japanese Management: The Cultural Background.' *Monumenta Nipponica*, 21(1–2): 47–60.

Brzezinski, Zbigniew K. (1972) *The Fragile Blossom.* New York: Harper & Row.

Bunka no Jidai Kenkyū Gurūpu. (1980) *Bunka no Jidai* (The age of culture). Tokyo: Japan Ministry of Finance Printing Bureau.

Burke, Ardath W. (1980) *Japan: Profile of a Postindustrial Power.* Boulder, CO: Westview.

Caldarola, Carlo. (1979) *Christianity: The Japanese Way.* Leiden, the Netherlands: Brill.

Cannadine, David. (1983) 'The Context, Performance and Meaning of Ritual: The British Monarchy and the Invention of Tradition, c. 1820–1977.' In *The Invention of Tradition*, eds. Eric Hobsbawm and Terence Ranger. Cambridge, England: Cambridge University Press, pp. 101–164.

Chiba, Tokuya, ed. (1980) *Nihon Minzoku Fūdo-ron* (The Japanese people and the environment). Tokyo: Kōbunsha.

Chikamatsu, Yoshiyuki. (1978) 'Fūdo to bungaku' (Environment and literature). In *Fūdogaku Joron* (Introduction to environment and culture), ed. H. Yamada. Tokyo: Tosho Kankōkai, pp. 153–172.

Chikushi, Tetsuya. (1982) *Sekai no Nihonjin-kan* (Views on the Japanese around the world). Tokyo: Jiyū Kokuminsha.

Chin, Shunshin. (1971) *Nihonjin to Chūgokujin* (The Japanese and the Chinese). Tokyo: Shōdensha.

Christopher, Robert. (1983) *The Japanese Mind: Goliath Explained.* New York: Simon & Schuster.

Chung, In-Wha. (1987, September) 'Sōru no atsui natsu' (A hot summer in Seoul). *Shokun*, pp. 104–111.

Chūō Daigaku Daigakuin Sōgō Seisaku Kenkyūka Nihonron Iinkai, ed. (2000) *Nihonron: Sōgō Seisaku e no Michi* (*Nihonjinron*: The road to comprehensive policy). Tokyo: Chūō Daigaku Shuppankai.

Coleman, John A. (1970) 'Civil Religion.' *Sociological Analysis*, 31: 67–77.

Dale, Peter. (1986) *The Myth of Japanese Uniqueness.* London: Croom Helm.

Davis, Winston. (1973) *Civil Religion in Modern Japan.* Ph.D. Dissertation, University of Chicago.

......... (1976) 'Civil Theology of Watsuji Tetsurō.' *Japanese Journal of Religious Studies* 3: 5–40.

......... (1983) 'The Hollow Onion: The Secularization of the Japanese Civil Religion.' In *The Challenge of Japan's*

*Internationalization: Organization and Culture*, eds. H. Mannari and H. Befu. Nishinomiya: Kwansei Gakuin University, pp. 212–231.

......... (1992) *Japanese Religion and Society: Paradigm of Structure and Change*. Albany: State University of New York Press.

De Tocqueville, Alex. (1954 [1835, 1840]) *Democracy in America*. 2 vols. New York: Vintage Books.

Denoon, Donald, et al. eds. (1996) *Multicultural Japan: Paleolithic to Postmodern*. Cambridge, England: Cambridge University Press.

Doi, Takeo. (1971) *'Amae' no Kōzō* (Anatomy of dependence). Tokyo: Kōbundō.

......... (1973) *Anatomy of Dependence*. New York and San Francisco: Kodansha International.

Edwards, Walter. (1989) *Modern Japan Through Its Wedding: Gender, Person, and Society in Ritual Portrayal*. Stanford, CA: Stanford University Press.

Egami, Namio. (1967) *Kiba Minzoku Kokka* (A nation of horseback riders). Tokyo: Chūō Kōronsha.

......... (1985) *Ajia: Minzoku to Bunka no Keisei* (Asia: Formation of its peoples and cultures). Tokyo: Nomura Shoten.

......... (1986) *Bunmei no Kigen to sono Seiritsu* (Origins and formation of civilization). Tokyo: Heibonsha.

Egami, Namio, et al. (1980) *Nihonjin to wa Nanika: Minzoku no Kigen o Motomete* (What is 'the Japanese'? In search of origins of the people). Tokyo: Shōgakkan.

Eisenstadt, S. N., and Eyal Ben-Ari, eds. (1990) *Japanese Models of Conflict Resolution*. London and New York: Kegan Paul International.

Endō, Shūsaku. (1969) *Silence*. Tokyo: Sophia University Press.

Etō, Jun, and Keiichirō Kobori, eds. (1986) *Yasukuni Ronsō* (The Yasukuni debate). Tokyo: Nihon Kyōbunsha.

Fawcett, Clare. (1995) 'Nationalism and Postwar Japanese Archaeology.' In *Nationalism, Politics, and the Practice of Archaeology*, eds. Philip L. Kohl and C. Fawcett. Cambridge: Cambridge University Press, pp. 232–246.

......... (1996) 'Archaeology and Japanese Identity.' In *Multi-*

*cultural Japan: Paleolithic to Postmodern*, ed. Donald Denoon. Cambridge: Cambridge University Press, pp. 60–77.

Fujitani, Takashi. (1996) *Splendid Monarchy: Power and Pageantry in Modern Japan*. Berkeley: University of California Press.

Fukasaku, Mitsusada. (1971) *Nihon Bunka oyobi Nihonjinron* (Japanese culture and *Nihonjinron*). Tokyo: San'ichi Shobō.

Fukuoka, Yasunori. (1993) *Zainichi Kankoku Chōsenjin* (Koreans in Japan). Tokyo: Chūō Kōronsha.

Furukawa, Yoshitaka. (1978) *Nihonjin no Kokoro no Rūtsu* (The roots of the heart of the Japanese). Tokyo: Kyōei Shobō.

Futaba, Kenko, and Masaki Umehara, eds. (1976) *Tennōsei to Yasukuni* (The Imperial institution and Yasukuni). Tokyo: Gendai Shokan.

Geertz, Clifford. (1963) 'The Integrative Revolution: Primordial Sentiments and Civic Politics in the New States.' In *Old Societies and New States*, ed. Clifford Geertz. New York: Free Press, pp. 105–157.

......... (1973) *Interpretation of Cultures*. New York: Basic Books.

Gehrig, Gail. (1981) *American Civil Religion: An Assessment*. Storry, CT: Society for the Scientific Study of Religion.

Gibney, Frank. (1979) *Japan, the Fragile Superpower*. New York: Norton.

Gluck, Carol. (1985) *Japan's Modern Myths: Ideology in the Late Meiji Period*. Princeton, NJ: Princeton University Press.

Goi, Masahisa. (1973) *Nihon no Kokoro* (The heart of Japan). Tokyo: Hakkō Shinkōkai Shuppankyoku.

Goldstein-Gidoni, Ofra. (1997) *Packaged Japaneseness: Weddings, Business and Brides*. Honolulu: University of Hawaii Press.

Gotō, Tetsuhiko. (1983) *Nihon-teki Keiei to Bunka* (Japanese-Style management and culture). Tokyo: Gakubunsha.

Hamaguchi, Eshun (or Esyun). (1977) *'Nihon Rashisa' no Saihakken* (The rediscovery of 'Japanliness'). Tokyo: Nihon Keizai Shinbunsha.

......... (1985) 'A Contextual Model of the Japanese: Toward a Methodological Innovation in Japanese Studies.' *Journal of Japanese Studies*, 2(2): 289–322.

......... (1996) *Nihon Bunka wa Ishitsuka* (Is Japanese culture heterogeneous?). Tokyo: Nippon Hōsō Shuppan Kyōkai.

......... (1998) *Nihon Shakai towa Nanika* (What is Japanese society?). Tokyo: Nippon Hōsō Shuppan Kyōkai.

Handelman, Don. (1990) *Models and Mirrors: Towards an Anthropology of Public Events*. Cambridge, England: Cambridge University Press.

Hanihara, Kazurō. (1995) *Nihonjin no Naritachi* (Formation of the Japanese people). Kyoto: Jinbun Shoin.

......... (1996) *Nihonjin no Tanjō* (Birth of the Japanese). Tokyo: Yoshikawa Kōbunkan.

......... (1997) *Nihonjin no Hone to Rūtsu* (Bones of the Japanese and their roots). Tokyo: Kadokawa Shoten.

Hanihara, Kazurō, ed. (1982) *Nihonjin wa Dokokara Kitaka* (Where did the Japanese come from?). Tokyo: Shōgakkan.

Hardacre, Helen. (1989) *Shinto and the State, 1868–1988*. Princeton, NJ: Princeton University Press.

Hasegawa, Nyozekan. (1938) *Nihon-teki Seikaku* (The Japanese character). Tokyo: Iwanami Shoten.

......... (1966) *The Japanese Character*. New York and San Francisco: Kodansha International.

Hayes, Carlton J. H. (1926) *Essays on Nationalism*. New York: Macmillan.

Hazama, Hiroshi. (1971) *Nihon no Keiei* (Management in Japan). Tokyo: Nihon Keizai Shinbunsha.

Higuchi, Kiyoyuki. (1974a) *Nihonjin Sai-Hakken* (Rediscovery of the Japanese). Tokyo: Bunken Shuppan.

......... (1974b) *Umeboshi to Nihontō: Nihonjin no Chie to Sōzō no Rekishi* (Dried plums and the Japanese sword: The history of Japanese wisdom and creativity). Tokyo: Shōdensha.

Hiro, Sachiya, and Shichihei Yamamoto. (1986) 'Yasukuni Shrine and the Japanese Spirit World.' *Japan Echo*, 13(2): 73–80.

Hisaeda, Kohei. (1976) *Keiyaku no Shakai Mokuyaku no Shakai: Nichi-Bei ni Miru Bijinesu Fūdo* (Contractual society and society of implicit agreement: Business environment in Japan and America). Tokyo: Nihon Keizai Shinbunsha.

Hobsbawm, Eric. (1983) 'Introduction: Inventing Traditions.' In *Invention of Tradition*, eds. E. Hobsbawm and Terence Ranger. Cambridge, England: Cambridge University Press, pp. 1–14.

Holtom, Daniel C. (1943) *Modern Japan and Shinto Nationalism*. Chicago: University of Chicago Press.

Holy, Ladislav, and Milan Stuchlik. (1981) 'The Structure of Folk Models.' In *The Structure of Folk Models*, eds. Ladislav Holy and Milan Stuchlik. New York: Academic Press, pp. 1–34.

Idemitsu, Sazō. (1971) *Nihonjin ni Kaere* (Return to being Japanese). Tokyo: Daiamondosha.

Ike, Nobutaka. (1978) *A Theory of Japanese Democracy*. Boulder, CO: Westview Press.

Ikumatsu, Keizō. (1963, January) 'Senzen no Nihon bunkaron.' (Pre-war *Nihonjinron*). *Shisō*, 463: 12–23.

Ikumatsu, Keizō, ed. (1977) *Nihonjinron* (*Nihonjinron*). Tokyo: Fuzanbō.

Inoue, Tetsujirō. (1891) *Chokugo Engi* (Lectures on the Imperial Rescript). Tokyo: Keigyōsha.

......... (1912) *Kokumin Dōtoku Gairon* (Outline of the national morality). Tokyo: Sanseidō.

Inuta, Mitsuru. (1977) *Shūdan Shugi no Kōzō: Nihon-teki Shūdan Shugi no Seishitsu to Koyō* (The structure of groupism: The characteristics of the Japanese groupism and employment). Tokyo: Sangyō Nōritsu Tanki Daigaku Shuppanbu.

Ishida, Eiichirō. (1969) *Nihon Bunkaron* (*Nihonjinron*). Tokyo: Chikuma Shobō.

......... (1974) *Japanese Culture: A Study of Origins and Characteristics*. Honolulu: University of Hawaii Press.

Ishigami, Ken. (1969) *Nihon no Kokoro* (The heart of Japan). Tokyo: Sekkasha.

......... (1971) *Zoku Nihon no Kokoro* (The heart of Japan, a sequel). Tokyo: Sekkasha.

Itagaki, Hiroshi. (1997) *Nihonteki Keiei: Seisan Shisutemu to Higashi Ajia* (Japanese-style management and East Asia). Kyoto: Minerva Shobō.

Itasaka, Gen. (1978) *Nihongo no Hyōjō* (Expressions of Japanese language). Tokyo: Kōdansha.

Itō, Mikiharu. (1995) *Zōyo Kōkan no Jinruigaku* (Anthropology of gift exchange). Tokyo: Chikuma Shobō.

Itoh, Mayumi. (2000) 'Japan's Neo-nationalism? Legislation of *Hinomaru* and *Kimigayo*.' Paper delivered at the annual meeting of the Association for Asian Studies, San Diego, California, March 9–12.

Itsui, Akihisa. (1973) *Nihon no Kokoro* (The heart of Japan). Tokyo: Hakkō Shinkō-kai Shuppan Honbu.

Itsuki, Hiroyuki, et al. (1992) *Nihonjin no Kokoro* (The heart of the Japanese). Tokyo: Kadokawa Shoten.

Iwasaki, Takaharu. (1980) 'Warera no uchi naru "mure-bito."' ('The mass' inside us). In *Shūdan Shugi* (Groupism), ed. E. Hamaguchi. Tokyo: Shibundō, pp. 31–41.

Iwata, Ryūshi. (1978) *Gendai Nihon no Keiei Fūdo* (Management environment in modern Japan). Tokyo: Nihon Keizai Shinbunsha.

Izumi, Seiichi and Masao Gamō. (1952) 'Nihon shakai no chiikisei.' (Regionalism in Japanese society). In *Nihon Chiri Shin Taikei* (A new compendium on the geography of Japan). Tokyo: Kawade Shobō, 2: 37–73.

Johnson, Frank. (1993) *Dependency and Japanese Socialization*. New York: New York University Press.

Kagono, Tadao. (1997) *Nihongata Keiei no Fukken: Monozukuri no Seishin ga Ajia o Kaeru* (Reassertion of the Japanese-style management: The spirit of manufacture changes Asia). Tokyo: PHP Kenkyūsho.

Kahn, Herman. (1970) *The Emerging Japanese Superstate: Challenge and Response*. Englewood, NJ: Prentice-Hall.

Kaizuka, Shigeki. (1974) *Nihon to Nihonjin* (Japan and the Japanese). Tokyo: Kadokawa Shoten.

Kakehi, Yasuhiko. (1984) *Nihongo to Nihonjin no Hassō* (Japanese lnaguage and the thought process of the Japanese). Tokyo: Nihon Kyōbunsha.

Kamei, Shunsuke. (1975) *Amerika no Kokoro Nihon no Kokoro* (The heart of America, the heart of Japan). Tokyo: Kōdansha.

Kamishima, Jirō. (1990) 'Society Convergence: An Alternative for the Homogeneity Theory.' *Japan Foundation Newsletter*, 17: 1–6.

Kamiya, Antonio. (1987) 'Nationalism: Is Japan Turning to Right?' *Intersect*, 3(2): 6–7, 10–11.

Kang, Sang-Choong. (1988, December) 'Nihonteki orientarizumu no genzai – kokusai ka ni hisomu hizumi' (Japanese-style Orientalism today: Hidden traps in internationalization). *Sekai*, pp. 133–139.

Kapferer, Bruce. (1988) *Legends of People, Myths of State*. Washington, D.C.: Smithsonian Institution.

Karaki, Junzō. (1965) *Nihon no Kokoro* (The heart of Japan). Tokyo: Chikuma Shobō.

Katō, Shūichi. (1976) *Nihonjin to wa Nanika* (What is 'Japanese'?). Tokyo: Kōdansha.

Kawai, Hayao. (1976) *Bosei Shakai Nihon no Byōri* (The pathology of Japan, a mother-complex society). Tokyo: Chūō Kōronsha.

......... (1984) *Nihonjin to aidentitī* (The Japanese and their identity). Tokyo: Sōgensha.

Kawai, Hayao, and Shin'ichi Nakazawa, eds. (1996–98) *Gendai Nihon Bunkaron* (Modern *Nihonjinron*). Tokyo: Iwanami Shoten.

Kawamoto, Akira. (1990) *Nihonjin to Shūdanshugi* (The Japanese and groupism). Tokyo: Tamagawa Daigaku Shuppanbu.

Kawamura, Nozomu. (1982) *Nihon Bunkaron no Shūhen* (Peripheries of *Nihonjinron*). Tokyo: Ningen no Kagakusha.

Kawashima, Takeyoshi. (1950) *Nihon Shakai no Kazoku-teki Kōsei* (Familial structure of Japanese society). Tokyo: Nihon Hyōronshinsha.

......... (1957) *Ideorogī toshiteno Kazoku Seido* (The family system as an ideology). Tokyo: Iwanami Shoten.

Kearney, Michael. (1984) *World View*. Novato, CA: Chandler & Sharp.

Kenmochi, Takehiko. (1978) *'Ma' no Nihon Bunka* (Pause in Japanese culture). Tokyo: Kōdansha.

......... (1980) *Hikaku Nihongaku no Susume* (Recommendation for comparative Japanology). Kyoto: PHP Institute.

Kim, Yong-Woo. (1983) *Kankokujin to Nihonjin* (The Koreans and the Japanese). Tokyo: Simul Shuppankai.

Kimata, Shin'ichi, and Mitsu Kimata. (1973) *Tsumetei Shakai Atatakai Shakai* (Cold society and warm society). Tokyo: Simul Shuppankai.

Kimata, Tokuo. (1978) 'Fūdo to shūkyō.' (Environment and religion). In *Fūdogaku Joron* (Introduction to environment), ed. H. Yamada. Tokyo: Tosho Kankōkai, pp. 173–192.

Kimura, Bin. (1972) *Hito to Hito to no Aida: Seishin Byōrigaku-teki Nihonron* (Interpersonal relationship: Pathological *Nihonjinron*). Tokyo: Kōbundō.

Kindaichi, Haruhiko. (1957) *Nihongo* (Japanese). Tokyo: Iwanami Shoten.

......... (1975) *Nihongo no Gengo Hyōgen* (Linguistic expressions in Japanese). Tokyo: Kōdansha.
......... (1977) *Nihongo no Tokushitsu* (Characteristics of Japanese). Tokyo: Kōdansha.
......... (1978) *The Japanese Language*. Rutland, VT: Tuttle.
Kitagawa, Tadaichi. (1983) *Nihonjin o Kangaeru: Kokuminsei no Dentō to Keisei* (Thinking on the Japanese: The tradition and formation of the national character). Tokyo: Nippon Hōsō Shuppan Kyōkai.
Kitayama, Shinobu, H. R. Markus, H. Matsumoto, and V. Norasakkunkit. (1997) 'The Individual and Collective Processes of the Construction of the Self: Self-Enhancement in the United States and Self-Criticism in Japan.' *Journal of Personality and Social Psychology*, 72: 1245–1267.
Kogawa, Tetsuo. (1988, October) 'Gaiatsu Seiji no Tasogare to Yasukuni.' (The dusk in foreign pressure politics and Yasukuni). *Sekai*, pp. 316–321.
Komatsu, Sakyō. (1977) *Nihon Bunka no Shikaku* (Deadly angle of Japanese culture). Tokyo: Kōdansha.
Konaka, Yōtarō. (1997) *Gaikoku no Kyōkasho ni Nihon wa dō Kakareteiruka* (How is Japan described in foreign school texts?). Tokyo: Goma Shobō.
Kōyama, Iwao. (1941) *Bunka Ruikeigaku Kenkyū* (A study in cultural taxonomy). Tokyo: Kōbundō Shobō.
Krauss, Ellis S., Thomas P. Rohlen, and Patricia Steinhoff, eds. (1984) *Conflict in Japan*. Honolulu: University of Hawaii Press.
Kuji, Toshitake. (1988) *Gendai no Kōkan Riron* (Modern exchange theory). Tokyo: Shinsensha.
Kuki, Shuzō. (1930) *'Iki' no Kozō* (The structure of *iki*). Tokyo: Iwanami Shoten.
Kunihiro, Masao. (1988) *Eigo Shikō to Nihongo Shikō* (English orientation and Japanese orientation). Tokyo: San'yūsha.
Kyōgoku, Jun'ichi. (1983) *Nihon no Seiji* (Politics in Japan). Tokyo: Tokyo University Press.
Lee, O-Young. (1982a) *'Chijimi Shikō' no Nihonjin* (Miniaturizing tendency of the Japanese). Tokyo: Gakuseisha.
......... (1982b) 'The Culture of Condensation.' *Japan Echo IX*(3): 95–104.

......... (1984) *Smaller Is Better: Japanese Mastery of the Miniature*. Tokyo and New York: Kodansha International.

Levi-Strauss, Claude. (1953) 'Social Structure.' In *Anthropology Today*, ed. Alfred L. Kroeber. Chicago: University of Chicago Press, pp. 524–553.

Lummis, Douglas C. (1981) *Uchi naru Gaikoku: 'Kiku to Katana' Saikō* (Foreigners within: Rethinking *The Chrysanthemum and the Sword*). Tokyo: Jiji Tsūshinsha.

Makino, Yoshiai, ed. (1995) *Nihon no Kokoro* (The heart of Japan). Tokyo: Kojinsha.

......... (1996) *Zoku Nihon no Kokoro* (The heart of Japan, a sequel). Tokyo: Kojinsha.

Maniwa, Mitsuyuki. (1990) *Nihon-teki Shūdan no Shakaigaku* (The sociology of the Japanese-style group). Tokyo: Kawade Shobō Shinsha.

Markus, H. R., and S. Kitayama. (1991) 'Culture and Self: Implication for Cognition, Emotion, and Motivation.' *Psychological Review*, 98: 224–253.

......... (1994) 'Collective Fear of the Collective: Implications for Selves and Theories of Selves.' *Personality and Social Psychology Bulletin*, 20(5): 568–579.

Maruyama, Yoshinobu. (1991) *Nihon no Kokoro* (The heart of Japan). Tokyo: Kindai Bungeisha.

Masuzoe, Yokichi. (1982) *Nihonjin to Furansujin* (The Japanese and the French). Tokyo: Kōdansha.

Matsubara, Hisako. (1985) *Nihon no Chie Yoroppa no Chie* (Japanese wisdom, European wisdom). Tokyo: Mikasa Shobō.

Miller, Roy Andrew. (1982) *Japan's Modern Myth: The Language and Beyond*. New York: Weatherhill.

Minami, Hiroshi. (1954) *Nihonjin no Shinri* (The psychology of the Japanese). Tokyo: Iwanami Shoten.

......... (1982) *Nihonjinron no Keifu* (The lineage of *Nihonjinron*). Tokyo: Kōdansha.

......... (1983) *Nihon-teki Jiga* (The Japanese self). Tokyo: Iwanami Shoten.

......... (1994) *Nihonjinron: Meiji kara Konnichi made* (*Nihonjinron*: From Meiji to today). Tokyo: Iwanami Shoten.

Minamoto, Ryōen. (1969) *Giri to Ninjō: Nihon-teki Shinjō no*

*Kōsatsu* (*Giri* and *Ninjō*: Investigation of the Japanese psychology). Tokyo: Chūō Kōronsha.

Minear, Richard H. (1980) 'Orientalism and the Study of Japan.' *Journal of Asian Studies*, 39(3): 507–517.

Misawa, Katsue. (1979) *Fūdoron* (Environment and culture). Tokyo: Misawa Shobō.

Miyagi, Otoya. (1969) *Nihonjin no Seikaku* (The character of the Japanese). Tokyo: Asahi Shinbunsha.

......... (1972) *Nihonjin to wa Nanika* (What is the Japanese?). Tokyo: Asahi Shinbunsha.

......... (1976) *Amerikajin to Nihonjin* (The Americans and the Japanese). Tokyo: Yamate Shobō.

Miyake, Setsurei. (1977) [1891] 'Shin Zen Bi Nihonjin' (Truth, goodness, and beauty in the Japanese) and 'Gi Aku Ki Nihonjin' (Deception, evil, and ugliness in the Japanese). In *Nihonjinron* (*Nihonjinron*), ed. K. Ikumatsu. Tokyo: Fuzanbō.

Miyamoto, Tsuneichi. (1967) *Fūdo to Bunka* (Environment and culture). Tokyo: Miraisha.

Morishima, Michio. (1977) *Igirisu to Nihon: Sono Kyōiku to Keizai* (England and Japan: Education and economy). Tokyo: Iwanami Shoten.

......... (1978) *Zoku Igirisu to Nihon: Sono Kokuminsei to Shakai* (England and Japan, a sequel: National character and society). Tokyo: Iwanami Shoten.

Motoyama, Yukihiko. (1958) 'Meiji nijūnendai no seiron ni arawareta nashonarizumu (Nationalism manifested in political theories of the Meiji twenties).' In *Meiji Zenhanki no Nashonarizumu* (Nationalism in the first half of the Meiji period), ed. Yoshio Sakata. Tokyo: Miraisha, pp. 37–84.

Mouer, Ross E. (1983) '"Orientalism" as Knowledge: Lessons for Japanologists?' *Keio Journal of Politics*, 4: 11–31.

Mouer, Ross, and Yoshio Sugimoto. (1986) *Images of Japanese Society*. London: Kegan Paul International.

Murakami, Katsutoshi. (1997) *Gaikokujin ni yoru Sengo Nihonron: Benedikuto kara Uorufuren made* (Postwar *Nihonjinron* by foreigners: From Benedict to Wolferen). Tokyo: Madosha.

Murakami, Yasusuke, Shunpei Kumon, and Seizaburō Satō. (1979) *Bunmei to shite no Ie Shakai* (Familial society as civilization). Tokyo: Chūō Kōronsha.

Nagashima, Yoshihiro. (1964) 'Nihon Bunka no Chiiki-teki Seikaku: Sonraku Shakai ni Kansuru Tōkei-teki Kenkyū' (Regionalism in Japanese culture: A statistical study of rural communities). *Jinrui Kagaku*, 16: 87–103.

Nakagawa, Nobuhiro. (1978) 'Nihon koso Sekai no Fukushi Chō-Taikoku da' (Japan, the welfare super-state). *Chūō Kōron*, 98(8): 86–103.

......... (1979) 'Japan, the Welfare Super-State. *Journal of Japanese Studies*, 5(1): 5–51.

Nagashima, Nobuhiro, and Hiroyasu Tomoeda, eds. (1984) 'Regional Differences in Japanese Rural Culture: Results of a Questionnaire.' *Senri Ethnological Studies*, 14 (A special issue).

Nakamura, Hajime. (1948–49) *Tōyōjin no Shii Hōhō* (Ways of thinking of Eastern peoples). 2 vols. Tokyo: Misuzu Shobō.

......... (1965) *Ways of Thinking of Eastern Peoples: India, China, Tibet, Japan*. Honolulu: East West Center Press.

Nakane, Chie. (1964, May) 'Nihon-teki shakai kōzō no hakken' (Discovery of the Japanese-style social structure). *Chūō Kōron*, pp. 48–85.

......... (1967) *Tate Shakai no Ningen Kankei: Tan'itsu Shakai no Riron* (Human relations in a vertical society: Theory of a homogeneous society). Tokyo: Kōdansha.

......... (1970) *Japanese Society*. Berkeley: University of California Press.

......... (1972) *Human Relations in Japan*. Tokyo: Ministry of Foreign Affairs.

Nakanishi, Susumu. (1997) *Nihonjin to wa Nanika* (What is the Japanese?). Tokyo: Kōdansha.

Nakao, Sasuke, and Kōmei Sasaki. (1992) *Shōyō Jurin Bunka to Nihon* (Culture in a forest of trees with shiny leaves and Japan). Tokyo: Kumon.

Nakazawa, Seiko. (1995) *Nihon no Kokoro: Kyōiku no Sekai kara* (The heart of Japan: From the world of education). Tokyo: Kindai Bungeisha.

National Diet Library, Research and Legislative Reference Department. (1976) *Yasukuni Jinja Mondai Shiryōshū* (Source materials for Yasukuni Shrine issues). Tokyo: National Diet Library.

Natsume, Sōseki. (1927) Kusamakura *and* Bunchō. Tokyo: Iwanami Shoten.

NHK Hōsō Yoron Chōsajo, ed. (1979) *Nihonjin no Kenminsei: NHK Zenkoku Kenmin Ishiki Chōsa* (Prefectural characteristics of the Japanese: NHK national survey of prefectural differences of self and other images). Tokyo: Nippon Hōsō Shuppan Kyōkai.

Nieda, Rokusaburō. (1975) *Nihonjin Jishin: Nihon Bunka ni Miru sono Jitsuzō* (The Japanese themselves: The reality as seen in Japanese culture). Tokyo: Yomiuri Shinbun.

Nihon Jinbun Kagakkai, ed. (1953) *Shakaiteki Kinchō no Kenkyū* (A study in social tension). Tokyo: Yūhikaku.

Nihon Shoseki Shuppan Kyōkai, ed. (2000) *Nihon Shoseki Sōmokuroku* (Books in print). Tokyo: Nihon Shoseki Shuppan Kyōkai.

Nishida, Kitarō. (1940) *Nihon Bunka no Mondai* (Problems of Japanese culture). Tokyo: Iwanami Shoten.

Nishida, Kōzō. (1978) *Nihon-teki Keiei to Hataraki-gai* (Japanese-style management and work motivation). Tokyo: Nihon Keizai Shinbunsha.

Noda, Masa-aki. (1988, March) 'Kanashii Shōchō – Okinawa to Hinomaru' (Sad symbols: Okinawa and the Hinomaru). *Shokun*, pp. 252–276.

Nomura Sōgō Kenkyūjo, ed. (1978) *Nihonjinron* (NRI Reference No. 2). Kamakura: Nomura Sōgō Kenkyūjo.

Nosco, Peter. (1990) *Remembering Paradise: Nativism and Nostalgia in Eighteenth Century Japan*. Cambridge, MA: Harvard University Council on East Asian Studies.

Numa, Shōzō. (1991a) *Kachikujin Yapū (1)* (Yapoo, the domesticated cattle: I). Tokyo: Sukora.

......... (1991b) *Kachikujin Yapū (2)* (Yapoo, the domesticated cattle: II). Tokyo: Mirion.

Odaka, Kunio. (1981) *Sangyō Shakaigaku Kōgi* (Lectures on industrial sociology). Tokyo: Iwanami Shoten.

......... (1984) *Nihon-teki Keiei: Sono Shinwa to Genjitsu* (Japanese-style management: Its myth and reality). Tokyo: Chūō Kōronsha.

Ōe, Shinobu. (1984) *Yasukuni Jinja* (Yasukuni shrine). Tokyo: Iwanami Shoten.

Oguma, Eiji. (1995) *Tan'itsu Minzoku Shinwa no Kigen* (Origins of the myth of a homogeneous nation). Tokyo: Shin'yōsha.

Ōide, Akira. (1965) *Nihongo to Ronri: Sono Yūkō na Hyōgen* (Japanese and logic: Its effective expressions). Tokyo: Kōdansha.

Okada, Susumu. (1972) *Nihonjin no Imēji Kōzō* (The image structure of the Japanese). Tokyo: Chūō Kōronsha.

Okada, Yasuhiro, and Shūzō Koyama, eds. (1996) *Jōmon Kandan: Sannai Daimaru no Sekai* (Jōmon Triad discussion: The world of Sannai Daimaru). Tokyo: Yamakawa Shuppansha.

Okazaki, Kimiyoshi. (1981) *Nihon no Kokoro no Shinsō Shinri: Nihon Bungaku Bunkaron no Tenkai* (The depth psychology of the heart of Japan: Development of the *Nihonjinron* of Japanese literature). Tokyo: Shinjusha.

Okonogi, Keigo. (1982) *Nihonjin no Ajase Konpurekkusu* (The Ajase complex of the Japanese). Tokyo: Chūō Kōronsha.

Ōno, Susumu. (1957) *Nihongo no Kigen* (Origins of Japanese). Tokyo: Iwanami Shoten.

......... (1974) *Nihongo o Sakanoboru* (Backtracking Japanese). Tokyo: Iwanami Shoten.

......... (1981) *Nihongo to Tamīrugo* (Japanese and Tamil languages). Tokyo: Shinchōsha.

Ōnuma, Yasuaki. (1986) *Tan'itsu Minzoku Shakai no Shinwa o Koete* (Transcending the myth of a homogeneous people). Tokyo: Tōshindō.

Pyle, Kenneth B. (1969) *The New Generation in Meiji Japan: Problems of Cultural Identity: 1885–1895*. Stanford, CA: Stanford University Press.

Reischauer, Edwin O. (1950) *The United States and Japan*. Cambridge, MA: Harvard University Press.

......... (1978) *The Japanese*. Cambridge, MA: Belknap Press.

......... (1979) *Za Japanīzu* (The Japanese). Tokyo: Bungei Shunjūsha.

......... (1988) *The Japanese Today: Change and Continuity*. Cambridge, MA: Belknap Press.

Richey, Russell E., and Donald G. Jones. (1974) *American Civil Religion*. New York: Harper & Row.

Rohlen, Robert. (1974) *For Harmony and Strength*. Berkeley: University of California Press.

Sabata, Toyoyuki. (1964) *Nihon o Minaosu: Sono Rekishi to Kokuminsei* (Reevaluating Japan: Its history and national character). Tokyo: Kōdansha.

......... (1972) *Bunmei no Jōken: Nihon to Yōroppa* (Conditions of civilization: Japan and Europe). Tokyo: Kōdansha.

......... (1974) *Bunmei to Fūdo* (Civilization and environment). Tokyo: Nihon Keizai Shinbunsha.

......... (1979) *Nikushoku Bunka to Beishoku Bunka* (Meat-eating culture and rice-eating culture). Tokyo: Kōdansha.

Said, Edward. (1978) *Orientalism*. New York: Random House.

Saitō, Makoto. (1972) *'Yamato-Damashī' no Bunka Shi* (Cultural history of the Japanese spirit). Tokyo: Kōdansha.

......... (1980) *Nihonjin to Sakura* (The Japanese and cherry blossoms). Tokyo: Kōdansha.

Sakata, Makoto. (1999) *Shin Daihyōteki Nihonjin* (The new representative Japanese). Tokyo: Shōgakkan.

Sakata, Yoshio, ed. (1958) *Meiji Zenhanki no Nashonarizumu* (Nationalism in the first half of the Meiji period). Tokyo: Miraisha.

Sapir, Edward. (1949) *Selected Writings in Language, Culture and Personality*, ed. David G. Mandelbaum. Berkeley: University of California Press.

Satō, Yoshirō. (1997) *Firipin no Rekishi Kyōkasho kara Mita Nihon* (Japan as seen from Philippine history texts). Tokyo: Akashi Shoten.

Seiyama, Kazuo, et al., eds. (2000) *Nihon no Kaisō Shisutemu* (Stratification system in Japan), 6 vols. Tokyo: Tokyo University Press.

Sekiguchi, Takeshi. (1983) *Kishō to Bunka* (Climate and culture). Tokyo: Tōyō Keizai Shinpōsha.

Sera, Masatoshi. (1965) *Nihonjin no Kokoro* (The heart of the Japanese). Tokyo: Nippon Hōsō Shuppan Kyōkai.

Shimizu, Ikutarō. (1968) *Nihon-teki naru mono* (That which is Japanly). Tokyo: Ushio Shuppansha.

Shimojima, Tetsurō. (1984) *Painukaji no Fuku Hi – Okinawa Yomitan Mura Shūdan Jiketsu* (The day the Painukaji Wind blew: The mass suicide in Yomitan, Okinawa). Tokyo: Dōshinsha.

......... (1988, March) 'Sanjū-hachi-nen-kan bokura wa nani o shiteita no darō – 'Hinomaru yakisute jiken' no oku ni aru mono.' (What have we been doing the last thirty-eight years? – That which is behind the flag-burning incident). *Shokun*, pp. 241–251.

Shin-Nihon Seitetsu Kōhō Kikaku-shitsu, ed. (1984) *Nihon: Sono Sugata to Kokoro* (Japan: Its reality and its heart). Tokyo: Gakuseisha.

......... (1987) *Nihon no Kokoro: Bunka Dentō to Gendai* (The heart of Japan: Culture, tradition, and the modern). Tokyo: Maruzen.

......... (1992a) *Nihon no Kokoro: Bunka to Dentō* (The heart of Japan: Culture and tradition). Tokyo: Maruzen.

......... (1992b) *Nihon no Kokoro: Gendai Shakai* (The heart of Japan: Modern society). Tokyo: Maruzen.

Shinohara, Hajime. (1968) *Nihon no Seiji Fūdo* (The political environment of Japan). Tokyo: Iwanami Shoten.

Shirayanagi, Shūko. (1938) (The Japanese people and the nature) Tokyo: Chikura Shobō

Smith, Robert J. (1961) 'The Japanese Rural Community: Norms, Sanctions, and Ostracism.' *American Anthropologist*, 63(3): 522–533.

......... (1983) *Japanese Society*. Cambridge, England: Cambridge University Press.

Sofue, Takao. (1971) *Kenminsei: Bunka Jinruigaku-teki Kōsatsu* (Prefectural characters: An anthropological study). Tokyo: Chūō Kōronsha.

......... (2000) *Kenminsei no Ningengaku* (The human science of prefectural characteristics). Tokyo: Shinchōsha.

Sugimoto, Yoshio. (1999) 'Making Sense of *Nihonjinron*.' *Thesis Eleven*, 57: 81–96.

Suzuki, Daisetz. (1938) *Zen Buddhism and Its Influence on Japanese Culture*. Kyoto: Eastern Buddhist Society.

......... (1940) *Zen to Nihon Bunka* (Zen and Japanese culture). Tokyo: Iwanami Shoten.

......... (1959) *Zen and Japanese Culture*. New York: Pantheon.

Suzuki, Hideo. (1975) *Fūdo no Kōzō* (The structure of environment). Tokyo: Kōdansha.

......... (1978) *Shinrin no Shikō Sabaku no Shikō* (Thought in forest, thought in desert). Tokyo: Nippon Hōsō Shuppan Kyōkai.

Suzuki, Takao. (1980) 'Gengo seikatsu' (Language life). In *Nihonjin no Ningen Kankei Jiten* (The dictionary of human relations among the Japanese), ed. Hiroshi Minami. Tokyo: Kōdansha, pp. 346–365.

Suzuki, Takao, Rokusaburo Nitoda, and Masamitsu Kawakami. (1983) *Nihonjin – Sono Gengo Shūkyō Dokusōsei* (The Japanese: Their language, religion, and creativity). Tokyo: Nihon Nōritsu Kyōkai.

Takano, Yōtarō, and Eiko Ōsaka. (1997) 'Nihonjin no shūdan shugi to Amerikajin no kojin shugi.' (The groupism of the Japanese and the individualism of Americans) *Shinrigaku Kenkyū*, 68: 312–327.

.......... (1999) 'An Unsupported Common View: Comparing Japan and the U.S. on Individualism/Collectivism.' *Asian Journal of Social Psychology*, 2(3): 311–341.

Takeuchi, Kumiko. (1999) *Parasaito Nihonjinron* (Parasite *Nihonjinron*). Tokyo: Bungei Shunjūsha.

Tamaki, Akira. (1978) *Inasaku Bunka to Nihonjin* (Rice culture and the Japanese). Tokyo: Gendai Hyōronsha.

Tanaka, Yoshitafu. (1924) *Kokumin Dōtoku Yōryō Kōgi* (Lectures on the principles of national morality). Tokyo: Nihon Gakujutsu Kenkyūkai.

Tanikawa, Tetsuzō. (1940) *Nihonjin no Kokoro* (The heart of the Japanese). Tokyo: Iwanami Shoten.

.......... (1947) *Bunkaron* (*Nihonjinron*). Tokyo: Kinbundō.

Terai, Minako. (1979) *Hitotsu no Nihon Bunkaron* (A certain *Nihonjinron*). Tokyo: Kōdansha.

Tornianen, Minna. (2000) 'From Austere Wabi to Golden Wabi: Philosophical and Aesthetic Aspects of Wabi in the Way of Tea.' *Studia Orientalia*, 90. Helsinki: Finnish Oriental Society.

Toyama, Shigehiko. (1973) *Nihongo no Ronri* (The logic of Japanese). Tokyo: Chūō Kōnronsha.

.......... (1976) *Nihongo no Kosei* (Characteristics of Japanese). Tokyo: Chūō Kōnronsha.

Trigger, Bruce. (1989) *A History of Archaeological Thought*. Cambridge, England: Cambridge University Press.

Tsuda, Masumi. (1977) *Nihon-teki Keiei no Ronri* (The logic of Japanese-style management). Tokyo: Chūō Kōnronsha.

.......... (1982) *Nihon-teki keiei no Shinro: Keieisha e no Isho* (The road to Japanese-style management: Will to be left for business managers). Tokyo: Chūō Keizaisha.

Tsukiyama, Jisaburō. (1972) *Fūdo to Rekishi* (Environment and history). Tokyo: Sōgensha.

Tsukuba, Hisaharu. (1969) *Beishoku Nikushoku no Bunmei* (Rice-eating and meat-eating civilizations). Tokyo: Nippon Hōsō Shuppan Kyōkai.

Tsunoda, Tadanobu. (1978) *Nihonjin no Nō: Nō no Hataraki to Tōzai no Bunka* (The Japanese brain: The workings of the brain and cultures East and West). Tokyo: Taishūkan.

Tsurumi, Shunsuke. (1996) *Nihonjin to wa Nandarōka* (What is 'the Japanese'?). Tokyo: Shōbunsha.

Tsurumi, Shunsuke, ed. (1997) *Nihonjin no Kokoro: Gen-Fūkei o Tazunete* (The heart of the Japanese: In search of the primal landscape). Tokyo: Iwanami Shoten.

Uchida, Roan. (1968) 'Rokumeikan jidai.' (The Rokumeikan period). In *Gendai Nihon Kiroku Zenshū* (Documentary compendium on modern Japan), ed. Senuma Shigeki. Vol. 4: *Bunmei Kaika* (Civilization and enlightenment). Tokyo: Chikuma Shobō, pp. 23–31.

Uchimura, Kanzō. (1908a) *Japanische Charaktersopse: Rechtmassige Verdeutschung* (Representative men of Japan). Stuttgart: D. Gundert.

......... (1908b) *Daihyōteki Nihonjin* (Representative men of Japan). Tokyo Iwanami Shoten.

......... (1941) *Daihyōteki Nihonjin* (Representative men of Japan). Tokyo Iwanami Shoten.

Ueyama, Shunpei. (1971) *Nihon no Shisō: Dochaku to Ōka no Keifu* (Japanese thought: The genealogy of indigenous and Europeanized thoughts). Tokyo: Simul Shuppankai.

......... (1980) *Nihon no Kokkazō* (The image of the Japanese nation). Tokyo: Nippon Hōsō Shuppan Kyōkai.

Ueyama, Shunpei, Komei Sasaki, and Sasuke Nakao. (1976) *Shōyō Jurin Bunka: Higashi Ajia Bunka no Genryū* (Culture in the shiny-leafed forest: Origins of East Asian culture). Tokyo: Chūō Kōronsha.

Umehara, Takeshi. (1976) *Nihon Bunkaron* (*Nihonjinron*). Tokyo: Kōdansha.

......... (1984) *Ainu wa Gen-Nihonjin ka: Atarashī Nihonjinron no tameni* (Are the Ainu proto-Japanese? Toward a new *Nihonjinron*). Tokyo: Shōgakkan.

Umehara, Takeshi, ed. (1990) *Nihon towa Nani nanoka* (What is Japan?). Tokyo: Nippon Hōsō Shuppan Kyōkai.

Umesao, Tadao, et al., eds. (1974) *Nihonjin no Kokoro: Bunka Miraigaku e no Kokoromi* (The heart of the Japanese: An attempt at cultural futurology). Tokyo: Asahi Shuppansha.

Urabe, Kuniyoshi. (1978) *Nihon-teki Keiei o Kangaeru* (Thinking about Japanese-style management). Tokyo: Chūō Keizaisha.

Usui, Yoshimi. (1984, June 2) 'Yamamoto Ben Dasan ni damasareta Nihonjin (1): Intābiu – Yamamoto Shichihei ni kiku.' (The Japanese were fooled by Yamamoto BenDasan (1): Interview – Listening to Yamamoto Shichihei). *Asahi Jānaru*, pp. 6–7.

Vogel, Ezra. (1979a) *Japan as Number One: Lessons for America.* Cambridge, MA: Harvard University Press.

········· (1979b) *Japan azu Nanbā Wan* (Japan as number one). Tokyo: TBS Britanica.

Wakamori, Tarō. (1981) 'Nihonjin no Kokoro' (The heart of the Japanese). In *Wakamori Tarō Chosaku-shū* (Collected works of Wakamori Tarō), vol. 8. Tokyo: Kōbunkdō.

Warner, William Lloyd. (1961) *The Family of God: A Symbolic Study of Christian Life in America.* New Haven, CT: Yale University Press.

Watanabe, Shōichi. (1973) *Nihonshi kara Mita Nihonjin: Aidentitī no Nihonshi* (The Japanese as seen from history: History of identity). Tokyo: Sangyō Nōritsu Daigaku Shuppanbu.

········· (1975, November) 'Kibagata Kokka to Nōkōgata Kokka.' (The Equestrian Type Nation and the Agrarian Type Nation). *Shokun*, 7: 22–45.

Watsuji, Tetsurō. (1935) *Fūdo: Ningengaku-teki Kōsatsu* (Climate: A humanological study). Tokyo: Iwanami Shoten.

········· (1961) *A Climate: A Philosophical Study.* Tokyo: Government Printing Bureau.

········· (1988) *Climate and Culture.* New York: Greenwood Press.

Weiner, Michael, ed. (1997) *Japan's Minorities: The Illusion of Homogeneity.* London and New York: Routledge.

Whorf, Benjamin. (1956) *Language, Thought, and Reality*, ed. John B. Carroll. Cambridge: Technology Press of Massachusetts Institute of Technology.

Wolferen, Karel. (1989) *The Enigma of Japanese Power: People and Politics in a Stateless Nation.* New York: Knopf.

......... (2000) *Okore! Nihon no Chūryū Kaikyū* (Middle class of Japan, get angry!) Tokyo: Mainichi Shinbun.

Yamada, Hideyo, ed. (1978) *Fūdoron Josetsu* (Introduction to environment). Tokyo: Kokusho Kankōkai.

Yamamoto, Shichihei. (1983) *Kūki no Kenkyū* (A study in 'air'). Tokyo: Bungei Shunjū.

......... (1992) *Nihonjin to wa Nanika* (What is the Japanese?), 2 vol. Kyoto: PHP Institute.

......... (1997) *Nihonkyōto* (*The Nihonkyō* faithful). Tokyo: Bungei Shunjū.

Yamamoto, Shichihei, and Naoki Komuro. (1981) *Nihonkyō no Shakaigaku* (The sociology of *Nihonkyō*). Tokyo: Kōdansha.

Yamashita, Hideo. (1979) *Nihon no Kotoba to Kokoro: Gengo Hyōgen ni Hisomu Nihonjin no Shinsō Shinri o Saguru* (The language and the heart of Japan: Exploration of the depth psychology hidden in linguistic expressions). Tokyo: Kōdansha.

Yanagita, Kunio. (1954) *Nihonjin* (The Japanese). Tokyo: Mainichi Shinbunsha.

Yasuda, Yojūrō, and Kōichi Nakagawa. (1969) *Nihonjin no Kokoro: Kokoro no Taiwa* (The heart of the Japanese: Conversation with the heart). Tokyo: Nihon Sono Sābisu Sentā.

Yoneyama, Toshinao. (1976) *Nihonjin no Nakama Ishiki* (Camaraderie among the Japanese). Tokyo: Kōdsansha.

Yoshida, Akihiko. (1996) *Nihonjin no kokoro: Kankyodō no Susume* (The heart of the Japanese: Recommendation of environmental way). Tokyo: Mirion Shuppan.

Yoshino, Kōsaku. (1992) *Cultural Nationalism in Contemporary Japan*. London: Routledge.

......... (1997) *Bunka Nashonarizumu no Shakaigaku* (The sociology of cultural nationalism). Tokyo: Nagoya Daigaku Shuppankai.

# Index

Europe,
 Japan compared to, 6, 19,
  23, 36, 38, 73–76, 105,
  123, 126, 128, 133, 136
 racial hierarchy, as part of, 75
European Association for
 Japanese Studies, x
exclusivity, Japan's, 21, 83–
  85, 116, 120

family, 15, 18–21, 25–26, 28,
  30–31, 37, 53, 60, 102,
  113, 115, 129, 132
 system,
  feudal nature of, 135–136
Fawcett, Clare, 41
feminism, 44–45
feudalism, 26, 124–126, 128,
  131, 134–138, 140
folk knowledge,
 Nihonjinron as, 76
folklore, 41
 Nihonjinron, as precursor to,
  16–17
foreigners, 24, 28, 46, 78–79,
  118, 127, 129
 Nihonjinron, authors of, 4,
  8–9, 49–52, 56–60
 Japan, and,
  inability to understand, 67,
   72, 109
  living in, 75–76, 82
  perceptions of, 56–57
frame, 11, 21, 107, 133
Fujimura, Shin'ichi, 42
Fujita, Tsugushi, 33, 88
Fujitani, Takashi, 88
Fukasaku, Mitsusada, 34, 48, 74
Fukuoka, Yasunori, 69

Fukutake, Tadashi, 135
Fukuzawa, Yukichi, 126
Furukawa, Yoshitake, 49
Futaba, Kenko, 99

Gamō, Masao, 70
Geertz, Clifford, 76, 83
Gehrig, Gail, 112, 113
gender, 4, 6, 44, 69, 71
genetic determinism, 69, 71–
  72, 75, 77, 133
genre,
 Nihonjinron as, 2–4
geoeconomics, 15, 63, 123–
  141
geography, 28, 71
 culture, effect on, 17, 134
geopolitics, 15, 63, 123–141
Gibney, Frank, 58
giri, 22, 73, 136
globalization, 33, 62, 82–83
glocalization,
 Nihonjinron, as expression
  of, 82
Gluck, Carol, 131–132, 144n
Goi, Masahisa, 32, 33, 49
Goldstein-Gidoni, Ofra, 114
Gotō, Tetsuhiko, 24–25
group model, 20, 22
group orientation, 5, 20–21,
  24, 28, 44, 60, 66, 73, 80
groupism, ix, 20–23, 27, 64,
  66, 74, 114, 123
 essentialism, and, 142n
 feminist perspective, lack of,
  44
 management style, as, 24–29
 paternalism within, 22–24,
 postwar changes to, 27

*wabi*, 25, 34
Wakamori, Tarō, 17, 32, 49
Warner, William, 112
Watanabe, Shōichi, 48, 74, 143n
Watsuji, Tetsurō, 7, 17–21, 24, 29, 32, 51, 74, 82, 114–115, 133–134, 142n, 144n
Weiner, Michael, 69, 84
West, the,
  denigration of, Japan's, 140
  Japan compared to, 6, 18–21, 60, 62, 68, 74–75, 81, 87–88, 125–132, 134, 136–140
  Other, as, 123
  rise of, 10–11
Western,
  admiration of Japan, 24
  criticism of Japan, 1
  culture,
    Japanese, compared to, 5–7, 39, 60, 66, 73–75, 81, 123, 125
  individualism, 5, 23, 27, 60, 73, 81
  languages, 36
  linguistics, 40
  management styles,
    Japanese, compared to, 27
  materialism, 102
  multiculturalism, 84
  *Nihonjinron*, authors of, 57–58
  pastoralism, 19–20,
  personality, 31
  philosophy, 144n
  scholars, 8
  views of Japan, 57–58
  war memorials, 98

westernization, 126–129
Whorf, Benjamin, 34–35
Wolferen, Karel, 122
World War II, 9, 30, 57, 74, 80, 86–88, 90–91, 93–95, 97–102, 114, 117, 121–124, 128–129, 135, 140–141

Yamada, Hideyo, 17
Yamamoto, Shichihei, 48, 51–52, 73, 81, 99, 105–113, 115–116, 142–144n. *See also* 80, Isaiah BenDasan
  humanology, concept of, 109–110
  nature, view of, 108
  *Nihonkyō*, concept of, 10, 105–112, 120, 122, 134–135
Yamashita, Hideo, 37
Yamazumi, Masaki, 96
Yanagita, Kunio, 16–17
Yasuda, Yojūrō, 33, 49
Yasukuni Shrine,
  religious symbolism of, 97–100
Yayoi period, 30, 43
Yomitan village,
  national flag, resistance to, 93–95, 100–101
Yoneyama, Toshinao, 23
Yosano, Akiko, 33
Yoshida, Akihiko, 32, 49
Yoshida, Shōin, 33
Yoshino, Kōsaku, 8, 12–14, 43, 54, 80
*yūgen*, 25, 81
Yukawa, Hideki, 54